Hidden Art

By the same author

L'ABRI

EDITH SCHAEFFER

HIDDEN ART

Illustrated by

DEIRDRE DUCKER

TYNDALE HOUSE PUBLISHERS
Wheaton, Illinois

*Library of Congress Catalog Card Number
70-123287. ISBN 8423-1420-2. Copyright © 1971
by Edith Schaeffer. All rights reserved.*

Seventh American printing, December 1975

*This Tyndale House edition published by
arrangement with The Norfolk Press, London,
England.*

Printed in the United States of America

ΠX 180 R4 S32 1972

The illustrations in Chapter 4 were drawn by the
author.

The drawing at the beginning of Chapter 9 contains
extracts used by kind permission of The Reader's
Digest Association Ltd, Oxford University Press, The
Evangelical Library and African Enterprise. 'Over in
the Meadow' from *My Book House* is included by
courtesy of Tangley Oaks Educational Center, Lake
Bluff, Illinois.

DEDICATED

TO

MY FAMILY

AND

THE L'ABRI FAMILY

Contents

1. The First Artist

What is Art? Authorities do not agree. Definitions differ.
Who draws the line that separates
   Art from Design?
   Sculpture from Ornaments?
   Poetry from Jingles?
   Great Music from Pooh's Hums?
   Great Literature from Daily News?

Is Art beauty, or depth, or expression?

Is Art communication calling for response?

Is Art the talent for involving other human beings in what otherwise would remain locked in the mind?

Is Art something that draws many into the beauty, joy and vividness of another person's understanding?

Is Art something that includes others in the torn struggling of another person's suffering?

Whatever it is, surely art involves *creativity* and *originality*. Whatever form art takes, it gives outward expression to what otherwise would remain locked in the mind, unshared. One individual personality has definite or special talent for expressing, in *some* medium, what other personalities can hear, see, smell, feel, taste, understand, enjoy, be stimulated by, be involved in, find refreshment in, find satisfaction in, find fulfilment in, experience reality in, be agonized by, be pleased by, enter into, but which they could *not* produce themselves.

Art in various forms expresses and gives opportunity to others to share in, and respond to, things which would otherwise remain vague, empty yearnings. Art satisfies and fulfils something in the person creating and in those responding.

One area of art inspires another area of art, but also one person's expression of art stimulates another person and brings about growth in understanding, sensitivity and appreciation. One active artist gives courage and incentive, and germinates ideas in others for producing more art. Hence a very poor, humble or unknown artist might easily provide the spark which kindles the fire of a great artist. But however good and great, his art is never perfect.

The only artist who is perfect in all forms of creativity – in technique, in originality, in knowledge of the past and future, in versatility, in having perfect content to express as well as perfect expression of content, in having perfect truth to express as well as perfect expression of truth, in communicating perfectly the wonders of all that exists as well as something about Himself, is of course God – the God who is Personal.

God, the Artist! We read in the New Testament in the book of Colossians: "For by him were *all* things created, that are in heaven, and that are in earth, visible and invisible." *All* things! Visible! The things my eyes can see – the poinsettia plants in Bermuda lanes and the blue gentians on Alpine paths, the deep brown eyes of a human friend, and the transparent green wings of

a grasshopper, the gnarled cypress of the California coast, and the orderly palms of Montreux's quay, the varied patterns of individual snow flakes, and the breathtaking beauty of a full moon lighting up snow-covered peaks and valleys. *All* things! Invisible! The things I know are there, but cannot see – wind and gravity, atoms and electrons, oxygen and sound waves. He also created beings visible to us – men; and beings invisible to us – angels.

God's Art communicates! We are told in the Old Testament in Psalm nineteen: "The heavens declare the glory of God; and the firmament showeth his handywork. Day unto day uttereth speech, and night unto night showeth knowledge. There is no speech nor language where their voice is not heard. Their line is gone out

through all the earth, and their words to the end of the world."
"The heavens *declare* the glory of God" – in these words we learn
that the whole of creation *communicates* something. More of creation can now be inspected as man brings some of the moon rock
back with him; more can be seen through a telescope or with the
naked eye – all that we see in the stars and the planets, the sun and
the moon. They are not only there for other useful reasons, but
also as an art form, a communication of the glory and the greatness
of the Artist. They communicate the wonder of who He is, and
what was in His mind as He created: not all of what was in His
mind, but something *truly* of what was in His mind.

"There is no language where their voice is not heard." In the
area of communication, language differences hinder at times.
Language hinders us when we wish to tell another human being
about the living God. Yet here we are told that from the beginning
of language differences, one thing continued which the lack of
language could not hinder. *The heavens continued to communicate
something to man*, something of the glory and wonder of God. The
heavens continue to declare to man something of the fact that He
is there. They testify that He exists, that He is the Supreme
Artist and the Perfect Scientist, who created the moon, and who
made the universe so precise in its composition and detail that
man could calculate with complete accuracy where two space ships
would meet in the depths of space. Why the precision of man's
calculations? Simply because the precision is *there* – it has been
created by the precise God.

So the heavens declare His glory: they *continue* to declare His
glory. They declared His glory in the time of the Babylonians;
they declared His glory when, at the Tower of Babel, the language
was suddenly different. Men could look up in their confusion of
human language difference, His glory was declared by what they
could see, and they could understand to the extent of the knowledge they possessed at that time. Today, five hundred million of
us in the world could sit before television sets, whether rented for

that special night in little mountain chalets, or in great mansions and palaces; whether in tier upon tier of flats or apartments, or out in the middle of Trafalgar Square; and *watch* the heavens declaring the glory of God as man stepped down on the moon. If only people realized it, they were watching a declaration that the Artist who had designed the moon in the first place had not made any miscalculations. His glory was being declared.

Psalm nineteen was written by King David, but years later Paul, another Jew, wrote in the Epistle to the Romans something that quotes David vividly. He is speaking of people hearing the Word, the communication, of God, and he goes on: "But I say, have they not heard? Yes verily, their sound went into all the earth, and their words unto the ends of the world." It echoes right back to that: "their words to the ends of the world." David wrote this with reference to the all-inclusive message of the creation which man can look up and *see* stretched out above him, night after starlit night, sunrise after flaming sunrise! The men of history, the people of all the centuries of human existence, have had before their eyes evidence of the Artist in whose mind these ideas first took shape, and who was able to express them in a visible form.

Little Margaret, my granddaughter, looked up at the ornamental plasterwork on the ceiling of the beautiful old ballroom in what is left of the original Ashburnham Place mansion in Sussex, England, where a recent L'Abri conference was held.

"Noni, what's all that fancy work up there? How was it made?"

I told her of the father of one of my college friends, Lou Volker, back in Philadelphia, who did ornamental plasterwork for ceilings of mansions in that city. It had gone out of style before he died. But as one looks at the intricate patterns on ceilings, made in another moment of history, and a child asks such a question, we do not answer, "Well! How interesting that plaster forty, sixty or eighty years ago formed itself into those interesting little patterns! It doesn't do that any more! Plaster has evolved now.

Plaster lies flat." Instead, we tell something of the artist who is behind it.

And this is what man is supposed to do. God gave him a mind that could logically work out that the heavens are declaring something, are communicating something: they are speaking of the glory of the Person who made them.

God has many art forms. My husband, Francis Schaeffer, has a lecture on God's use of art forms in the tabernacle and temple. But I want to point out some of God's art forms in His original creation.

"For, lo, he that formeth the mountains, and createth the wind, and declareth unto man what is his thought, that maketh the morning darkness, and treadeth upon the high places of the earth, The Lord, The God of hosts, is his name" (Amos 4: 13).

God was the first Sculptor. God *formed* the mountains, using a variety of stone textures (white marble near Pisa, grey granite, streaked terra cotta in the Grand Canyon, the green stone of Zermatt), and a variety of shapes, colours and forms. Of all the variety of God's sculpture, remember that He made the first human forms. Sculptors through the ages have found the human body the most beautiful form to work with. To capture with movement and individuality the human form in marble, clay or bronze has always been a challenge. But who made the human form in the first place? Who conceived it in the realm of the mind, of ideas, and then brought it forth into the visible world? The Sculptor – God.

But that second phrase – "and created the wind." We think of mobiles that modern man is making, mobiles that not only have form but movement, moving with the slightest breath of air. Here is the desire for movement in art!

Think of the mobiles of God, the Artist, brought forth by the wind that He created. The wind, blowing in the trees, swaying the grass, bending a field of wheat as a ballet, rising again, bending again. The spray of the ocean, wild waves against rocks bringing forth a curve of spray, a mobile of spray. Light through spray, like thousands of diamonds blowing on invisible threads! The movement of the birch trees' delicate branches and sensitive leaves twinkling and twisting, fluttering in a breeze; or clouds drifting slowly across a clear sky or scudding in swift movement as shapes change – God's mobiles.

It may be debated whether the modern light shows are an art form or not. Flashed on walls are changing colours and shapes, as reflected drops of oil on water change in form and size. Scenes that look like underwater views of the deep sea diver keep movement with music.

But – have you considered the light shows that God created? Watch the moon come up over the mountain, as first the light in the sky softens the dark, and then a copper arc appears and quickly changes into an enormous ball outlining the mountain and streaking the clouds with light. Watch it change in colour and size as it mounts in the sky.

Come out in the early morning for a more dramatic show, as the sun colours the sky with dark purples and reds before it can be seen, and then floods the mountain peaks with a halo of brilliance before it spills over warmth and light to the whole valley. Look at the streaks of lightning that split the black sky with zigzag patterns, or gasp over a northern light display. Watch a falling star cut through a night sky, and then look down over a cliff to the white foam bright in moonlight washing the rocks with black wetness. Swim in southern waters and open your eyes to the fish, a variety of shapes and colours flashing among sea weeds and coral. These are God's light shows!

Then think of sound. God created not only the sound, but He created ears to hear the sound. Have you ever thought of an *On the Beach* kind of ending to the world? With a tape recorder playing some gorgeous piece of your favourite music on a satellite going forever around in space. A poem being sung forever on another, with magnificent words and a wonderful voice. No ears to hear, no person to respond, no communication going on anywhere: just sound by itself, beautiful sound. It would be meaningless, wouldn't it?

God created sound, ears, and a capacity in man for the appreciation of music and a variety of sound. The capacity differs, of course. It differs between individuals just as sensitivity to other things differs, because we have been created as individual personalities, not as machines rolled out of a bigger machine. God is diverse in His creation of man, as well as in His creation of all other things. The unity and diversity is fantastic both in its variety and in the degrees of difference in man's capacity to appreciate. And yet, all men have *some* capacity to hear and to appreciate music. (Although, since creation was spoiled, illness or accident has cut off some people from hearing, as well as from seeing or speaking.) The songs of the birds were created by God. Their music has been captured in notes which violins have replayed, and other instruments have blended into symphonies. But who first created music? God the Composer. God the Musician.

We find in the Old Testament book of Job that stars once sang. God is asking Job, "Where wast thou . . . when the morning stars sang together, and all the sons of God shouted for joy?" Later God asks, "Knowest thou it, because thou wast then born? Or because the number of thy days is great?" Oh man, do you know so much because *you* have lived for millions or billions of years? Do you know all these things that make you feel so superior, so educated, so intellectual, because you have lived so long? How much research can you do in a lifetime, oh finite man? How much can you find out in the span of years you have left to you? I am telling you things that are not in your records, things I was there to see. And not only to see, but to think of and create in the first place.

There was once an opportunity to hear the music of stars: stars blended together in a *music*. What sort of music? I think we shall find out some day. God says it resembled song. Have you heard

'Switched-On' Bach? Electronic music? Have you heard a shepherd's flute, an Alpine horn or an African drum? There is a wide range of differing sounds in the realm of man's music, because God made a wide range possible. And – "the stars sang" – made *some* sort of music.

Revelation, the last book of the Bible, tells us in wording that makes it sound like past history although it has not yet taken place (John, the writer, was taken by God in a vision or in person to see what it would be like, so that he could write it): "And they sung a new song, saying, Thou art worthy to take the book, and to open the seals thereof: for thou wast slain, and hast redeemed us to God by thy blood out of every kindred, and tongue, and people, and nation; and hast made us unto our God kings and priests; and we shall reign on the earth." A marvellous day is coming when we shall sing with great joy about those events of past history which affect each one of us who will be there. This song will be sung together by some of every kindred, and tongue, and people and nation. Language will be no barrier. There will be complete integration. Heaven, eternal life, is not shut up to one family, national, or racial line, or one language root. Some from every single tribe and people will be there, singing together with true joy.

Oh yes, God makes it clear through the ages that there is only one way of being among these people, of being in His family – through the slain Lamb, but He also makes it clear that *some* from every group will be there. How many will be singing there? Revelation speaks of the gathering as "a great multitude which no man could number, of all nations, and kindreds, and people and tongues." There is singing and music which lie in the future – a beauty in the future too – designed, created and prepared by the same Artist whose work we have seen. True enough, all this work of His has been spoiled by sin in the universe, so we cannot fully know what the perfection of the future will be like. But He is the same Artist whose workmanship we have lived with, and enjoyed.

We may note here, in passing, the centrality of the element of pleasure, the importance of joy and response in the artistic realm that God created. In each of the art forms, the original Artist was God.

Now God has not only created all the variety of growing trees and flowers, shrubs and ferns, grasses and moss – things that grow and give us beauty. A place like Kew Gardens in London demonstrates something of the wonder and infinite variety of this 'art area' of the Creator God. But God was also the first landscape architect! In Genesis, the first book of the Bible, we read this:

"And the Lord God planted a garden eastward in Eden; . . . And out of the ground made the Lord God to grow every tree that is pleasant to the sight, and good for food." What a fantastic garden it must have been. God not only created all the flowers, trees, shrubs, ornamental plants and fruits to put in it, but He actually designed and *planted* a garden. He designed it so that it might contain things that were good to eat, but they were also to be *pleasant* to look at. It mattered enough to God that it should be beautiful to look at. God the Landscape Architect planned a garden, with absolutely perfect balance and symmetry, blending the variety with perfection. The number of paths and the curve of their windings through the growth would have been perfect for those evening walks together with Adam and Eve. The blending of colours and groupings of different heights of plants would have been perfect because they were planted by God – not just created by God, but *planted* by Him. God deemed it important to make a beautiful garden, artistic to the highest degree, taking what had already been made and arranging it as an artist would take his paintings and pieces of sculpture and group them for an exhibition, or as a musician would arrange the sequence of selections for an evening.

All of this leads up to the most important aspect of God's art, and one that concerns us personally: "And God said, Let us make man in our image, after our likeness: . . . So God created man in his own image, in the image of God created he him . . ."

Man was made *in the image of God*. But what is God like? In whose image is man made? Certainly, he is made in the image of a Person, so man is a person. God has all the marks of personality, so man is a personality, who can think, act and feel. Therefore man loves, because he has been given the capacity for love. He has been made in the image of One who has loved for ever and ever. (The Father has loved the Son, and the Holy Spirit. The Son has loved the Father and the Holy Spirit. The Holy Spirit has loved the Father and the Son.) Man can communicate because he was made in the image of God who communicates within the Trinity. Man has a capacity for communicating and receiving communication, for sharing with other human beings, and also with God. But the heart of the discovery is this: we are created in the likeness of *the Creator*. *We* are created in the image of a *Creator*.

So we are, on a finite level, people who can create. Why does man have creativity? Why can man think of many things in his mind, and choose, and then bring forth something that other people can taste, smell, feel, hear and see? Because man was created in the image of a Creator. Man was created that he might create. It is not a waste of man's time to be creative. It is not a waste to pursue artistic or scientific pursuits in creativity, because this is what man was *made* to be able to do. He was made in the image of a Creator, and given the capacity to create – on a finite level of course, needing to use the materials already created – but he is still the creature of a Creator.

But in creativity choice is involved. Why were we not made so that we could not do anything but *one* set of things which would have been absolutely good, and without sin? We were to have choice so that *love would have meaning*. Love could have no meaning without choice. (We would not wish to be loved by a robot that has been programmed to love us.) But more than that is involved. Something that is not mentioned very frequently by people speaking of the problem of 'choice' – and agonizing over why man had to have choice anyway, because of all the sorrow of sin and suffering – is one of the most central things involved in the principle of choice, and that is *creativity*. Creativity *involves* choice.

What is creativity? What is it we do when we create something? We start with an idea, or a number of ideas. Something comes into our minds. We have a flow of ideas, sometimes a tremendous flow of ideas, at times in one direction, or at other times in another direction; or perhaps even ten directions at once. *And we have to make a choice.* We cannot do everything that comes into our minds, nor can we create everything that comes into our imaginations, whether it be in a very great or complicated area of science or art, or in a very mundane area, such as whether we should make a chocolate, vanilla or spice cake for the evening meal. There is choice involved in the very simplest form of creativity, because as any set of possibilities comes into our minds, we have to choose.

Man, because he is limited, has a very limited choice. He is limited by time, as well as talent. He is limited by the resources at his disposal as well as in the skill to use what he has. We do not all have the talent to produce all the ideas that come into our minds. We might think of some very great idea. Boys and men thought of going to the moon many years ago, but no one had the talent or resources at that time actually to get there. A man might think of some great painting in his mind, but not be able to execute it on canvas at all, because he does not have the talent to paint.

But time is also involved. We each have a very limited number of hours in a day. Often I would like to add to those hours, but have never found a way to do it. There are just seven of those twenty-four-hour periods in a week, and a very limited number of weeks in a month, and there are only twelve months in a year. Then, how many years are there in a life? It really goes – like *that*! It does not take long to disappear.

And so – what can we get done in those few hours and days and weeks and years? We are limited by time and by areas of talent and ability. So our creativity is not on God's level at all. His creativity is unlimited and infinite. Nevertheless we have been created in His image, so we can be, and are *made* to be, creative.

Man has a capacity both for responding and producing, for communicating as well as being inspired. It is important to respond to the art of others, as well as to produce art oneself. It is important to inspire others to be creative as well as to communicate by one's own creative acts.

The next question would be: how is man's capacity for creativity, for art, to be used? Without sin, man would have been perfectly creative, and we can only imagine what he would have produced without its hindrance. With sin, all of God's creation has been spoiled to some degree, so that what we see is not in its perfect state. One day, God will restore all that has been destroyed or spoiled.

Before going on, it would be worth considering what Isaiah, an Old Testament prophet, said: "To appoint unto them that mourn in Zion, to give them beauty for ashes, the oil of joy for mourning, the garment of praise for the spirit of heaviness, that they might be called the trees of righteousness, the planting of the Lord: that he might be glorified."

God is capable of re-making and restoring that which has been spoiled, and He promises to do so. Primarily, of course, what excites us most in His promise to 'restore' (as injured paintings are restored, or spoiled buildings are restored) is man himself. He can make us into new creatures in Christ Jesus now; but He can also, one day, *restore* us and make us, physically and spiritually, what Christ was after His resurrection. We are told that we are going to have bodies like Christ's glorious body, and that we are going to live throughout eternity without sin. God is able to restore what has been spoiled in His creation, at every level.

However, those who believe there is a God and believe the Bible to be true, often leave out one important fact: that although creation and man have been spoiled by sin, there is left over in creation a glimpse of what God created in the first place. First, there remains the beauty of the whole universe, and of the heavens. The Psalmist tells us: "The heavens declare the glory of God . . ." So we can look out and see something that still declares His glory to us, even though sin has entered the world. We look at the trees and the mountains. We look at lakes and the variety of old oaks and evergreen trees, redwoods and weeping willows, and we see remnants of His creation which have not been spoiled. In another area of the world we see the sun setting behind the Alps, and the Alpine rouge coming on the snowy peaks and covering them all with rose, and we feel we are seeing something almost totally unspoiled. But on the other hand we can go to a place where there have just been hurricanes and tornadoes, and see not only houses crashed down and ruined, but a landscape with trees twisted and destroyed. As one stands in an area that has been hit by an earthquake or an avalanche the changed and destroyed earth is a shattering sight. Not all of the physical beauty of the world is equally spoiled, or equally unspoiled. But there are fragments of beauty to show the glory of the Creator, the Artist God.

But the same is also true in man, though again many Christians miss it. In man there are remnants of the beauty of what God created in the first place.

Those of us who are parents have probably had a child come to us and ask why it is that Mr. Q, who lives next door, and who is an atheist, is kinder, nicer, and more likeable than Mr. Z, who lives on the other side, and who is a Christian. "Aren't Christians supposed to be nicer than atheists?"

My answer is that there are some people who are physically much more healthy than others. Others have a beauty of face and form which seems almost perfect. There are also people who in character, sensitivity, gentleness, kindness, consideration, unselfishness, and so on, have been born with qualities which give glimpses, in certain areas of being, of what God made in the first place. Now I am *not* saying that people are born 'good'. And I am *not* saying that there is anyone who is without sin, because each of these persons is sinful in the sight of God, and has broken his own standards, as well as God's law, sinning against Him and against men in many areas. But nevertheless some men are as difficult to have for neighbours as others are kind and considerate. The only explanation seems to be the beauty of God's creation 'left over' in some people in some areas of their characters.

Now the same thing is true in the area of creative ability. Is every marvellous artist a Christian? No. But there is 'left-over' beauty in the creation of God. Since He created man as a creative creature, by creating him in His own image, these 'creative creatures' have, through the ages, retained fragments of the perfection which He made in the first place – though spoiled, of course, by sin. Every single one of us *has* been spoiled by sin. But as we look back over history and see artists, musicians and creative people in various fields, we can recognize the 'image of God'.

With this as a background, I would go on to ask the next question. Is a Christian – one who is in communication daily with the Creator (communication made possible because of redemption through the blood of Christ) – to divorce himself from the things God created and intended man to have, and which *demonstrate* the fact that man has been made in the image of God? In other words are we, who have been made in the image of our Creator, and who acknowledge and understand what that means because we know God exists, and experience communication with Him – are we to be less creative than those who do not know that the Creator made them in His image, and who have no contact with Him?

The First Artist

It seems to me that the marks of personality – love, communication, and moral sensitivity – which are meant to sharpen as we are returning to communication with God, should lead to an *increased* rather than a decreased creativity. The Christian should have more vividly expressed creativity in his daily life, and have *more* creative freedom, as well as the possibility of a continuing development in creative activities.

Before going on to the practical chapters of this book, I would put in a parenthesis: Christians have a capacity for spiritual communication with God. So we need to spend adequate time with Him, reading His communication to us and praying in intercession for others, and for our own needs. And of course we are limited by finiteness and our time is precious. Of course Christians have a responsibility to communicate truth to others who do not know it. These are all priorities, and such aspects of a healthy, growing Christian life are neither being ignored nor contradicted by what follows.

But, not forgetting the above, then what I call 'Hidden Art' should be *more* important to one who knows and admits that he is made in God's image, than to those who do not.

2. What is Hidden Art?

I would define 'Hidden Art' as the art which is found in the 'minor' areas of life. By 'minor' I mean what is involved in the 'everyday' of anyone's life, rather than his career or profession. Each person, I believe, has some talent which is unfulfilled in some 'hidden area' of his being, and which could be expressed and developed.

Because we are finite and limited, and because human beings are diverse, there must be a great diversity in the possibilities and opportunities of what I would call 'Hidden Art', but it should find a constantly growing and widening expression as life goes on. The

31

choice of the use of one's time will be deeply involved in it. I am not suggesting that everyone can include in his or her daily life all the ideas explored in these pages. That would be as impossible as doing any one thing perfectly. I am simply going to outline a few areas of life where I feel many of us could experience a greater personal fulfilment in creativity, and so enrich the lives of the people we live amongst.

All art involves conscious discipline. If one is going to paint, do sculpture, design a building or write a book, it will involve discipline in time and energy – or there would never be any production at all to be seen, felt or enjoyed by ourselves or others. To develop 'Hidden Art' will also, of course, take time and energy – and the balance of the use of time is a constant individual problem for all of us: what to do, and what to leave undone. One is always having to neglect one thing in order to give precedence to something else. The question is one of priorities.

It would be very frustrating if we expected each other to do each thing perfectly, or to add new creative things without eliminating something else. Of course something is being neglected every day. That is the finite bit of humanity asserting itself! But – and this needs emphasis – a Christian, above all people, should live *artistically, aesthetically, and creatively*. We are supposed to be representing the Creator who is there, and whom we *acknowledge* to be there. It is true that all men are created in the image of God, but Christians are supposed to be *conscious* of that fact, and being conscious of it should recognize the importance of living artistically, aesthetically, and creatively, as creative creatures of the Creator. If we have been created in the image of an Artist, then we should look for expressions of artistry, and be sensitive to beauty, responsive to what has been created for our appreciation.

Does this mean that we should all drop everything to concentrate on trying to develop into great artists? No, of course not. But it does mean that we should consciously do *something* about it. There should be a practical result of the realization that we have been created in the image of the Creator of beauty. Whether you are married and have a family; whether you share a house or a flat with one or a number of people; whether you still live with your parents; whether you live alone and have guests in from time to time; whether you are a man or a woman: the fact that you are a Christian should show in some practical area of a growing creativity and sensitivity to beauty, rather than in a gradual drying up of creativity, and a blindness to ugliness.

Courses of Art Appreciation, lectures on the History of Art, discussion of great art, and the explanation of what makes great music, can make many people feel discouraged, or even a bit resentful and bitter, feeling 'outside' the magic circle of the talented. We may think 'If only . . .' – If only I weren't so tied down with the mundane things of life. If only I had had a chance to go to art school. If only I had time to develop instead of being caught in this job. If only I hadn't this endless round of housework and crying babies to overwhelm me. 'If only . . .' feelings can distort our personalities, and give us an obsession which can only lead to more and more dissatisfaction, as well as making us into 'Eeyore-ish' and uncomfortable-to-be-with people!

It is not that I feel the study of great art should be put aside, but simply that I feel it may be helpful to consider some of the possibilities all of us have of really *living* artistically, but which are often ignored. People so often look with longing into a daydream future, while ignoring the importance of the present. We are all in danger of thinking, "Some day I shall be fulfilled. Some day I shall have the courage to start another life which will develop my talent", without ever considering the very practical use of that talent *today* in a way which will enrich other people's lives, develop the talent, and express the fact of being a creative creature.

Have you ever had a leg in a cast? When the cast comes off, there is a stiffness which it takes time to get rid of, but gradually with exercise the muscles and joints limber up again, and after a time the cast is forgotten and the freedom to run, ski, climb and swim develops more skill in the leg than before, and confidence and fulfilment come in the physical satisfaction of having the use of the leg which was idle so long.

For many people, and too often for many Christian people, the areas in which they could be creative have been encased in a cast, and the creative muscles and joints (if I can use that picture!) have stiffened with disuse. The purpose of the next pages is to help crack off the plaster and restore life to cramped limbs.

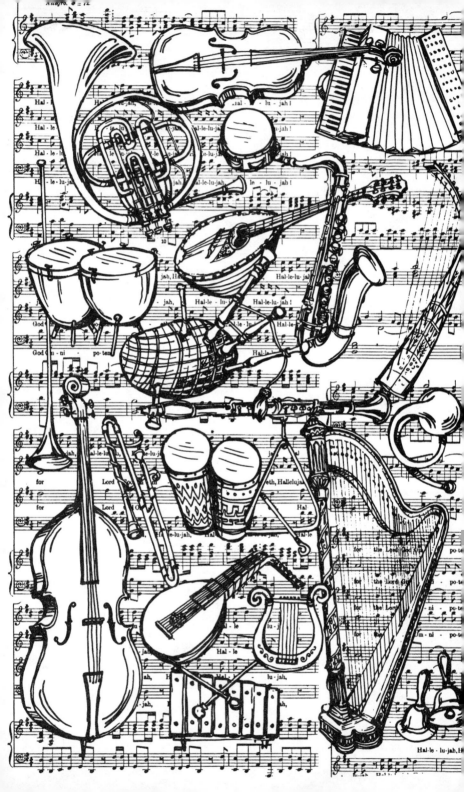

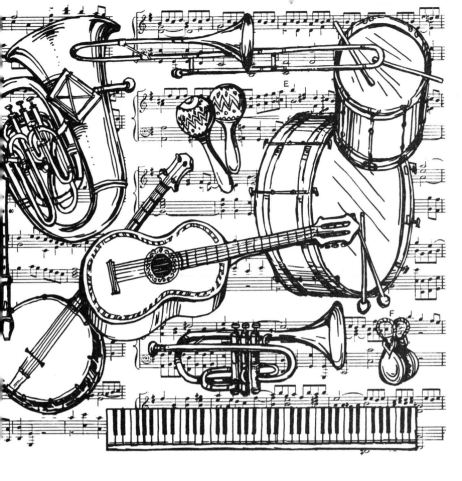

3. Music

You are not a great musician but you do play an instrument – or you did. It is dusty at present, because you could not go to a Conservatoire, you could not continue lessons, you have not found an organized group to play with, you are busy as a businessman, a gardener, a lawyer, a teacher, a housewife or a graduate student. All the music you make is in your daydreams of some remote future success, when you burst upon audiences as an established talent, or surprise your friends by letting them know you have been 'discovered'. Your musical talent and your creative possibilities are in a cast, and the rest of your body and personality are suffering from the lack of freedom. People working or living with you are affected by what is going on in you, and are also being deprived of what could be a shared thing.

Even if musical talent is 'just' used within a family, someone is appreciating what is being produced, or is sharing in the enjoyment of producing something together. In the family, with small children; among friends, informally for one's own expression as well as for other people's appreciation; for relaxation; for just plain fun and sharing; for the experience of doing something creative together – music should be a part of the life of any family or other group of people who have any musical talent at all. Not only will the practice improve one's playing, but creative ideas and imagination will be sparked off in others in a way which will be fulfilling and satisfying, even if it is not earth-shaking in its talent. In the process something else will happen – the freedom to express yourself in a medium that is yours will develop, and so will your personality. It will not be just a matter of your musical contribution making you more interesting to have around, but you will yourself be a more interesting person. It is very logical, really. Stifling or squashing a natural expression detracts from one's personality.

John Sandri comes from a musical family. His father is a Swiss businessman who has been busy for years in a time-consuming business which has taken him to many countries as well as all over Switzerland. Mrs. Sandri, as a mother and housewife, has also led a full life. John is the Treasurer of L'Abri, with lectures to prepare as well as all the L'Abri business to care for. Yet through the years when they have had a day, an afternoon or an evening together, the Sandri family has enjoyed producing music together. Mr. Sandri plays a violin, Mrs. Sandri the piano, and John the cello. They all could be in an orchestra – they play beautifully. But one would have to sneak up on them or eavesdrop to find this out. They play alone, with friends or other members of the family present only occasionally, because essentially they are enjoying music in the same way that others enjoy conversation and discussion, rather than as a performance. They go through chamber music scores together. They 'play along' with records which are prepared with certain instruments missing – for the purpose of giving musicians the opportunity of playing 'in' an orchestra, without having the orchestra present! And 'in between' they practise alone, for personal outlet as much as for anything. John sometimes keeps the cello by him in his tiny chalet office so that he can let off steam, or relax, in the midst of doing the frustrating monthly and yearly accounts of L'Abri for the Swiss *Fiduciare*.

Ranald Macaulay, who heads up the L'Abri work in England, often sits down to play Bach or Mozart to relax. But even more often, if you were a London sparrow on the windowsill of the L'Abri house in Ealing, you would hear Christopher Robin songs being sung to piano accompaniment, as Ran, with a tiny daughter on his knee, and another beside him, delights his children by singing with them. They sing hymns, too, and a whole repertoire of interesting songs. There is a charm in making music together which not only stimulates interest and creativity, but which breaks through whining and fussing and clears the atmosphere. This can be said for adults as well as children! Recorders or flutes, banjos or mandolins can be played together, and we can keep time with cymbals or by tapping lightly on a water glass.

This 'togetherness' in creating music can include the composition of original music, where there is the talent. And at the other end of the scale, families with no talent for producing music at any level can enjoy music 'appreciation' with a selected variety from a slowly growing collection of records to be listened to, studied, and discussed together. Occasional 'live' concerts should be added to the records or selected radio concerts. Children should be exposed to good music, whether it is being produced by parents, being heard together on a record-player and discussed, or performed in a concert hall.

Christian homes should not be places where nothing but a bit of sentimental or romantic music is heard, but places where there is the greatest variety of good music, so that natural talent may find the necessary spark to set it on fire. The natural inclination of small children to blow whistles and beat drums should be encouraged and led by parents, with some imaginative plan to lead on from the tuneless drum-beating into the next steps of music production. If you have no children of your own, you can adopt some for scattered hours in your life, helping them and yourself at the same time.

Do not be embarrassed to take along a violin or a flute to someone's home if you think there will be a time of singing around the piano. Your instrument will add variety to the voices and will enrich the experience of those singing, as well as provide you with an outlet for your talent. This also may encourage someone else to bring along an instrument another time. Instead of simply listening to professionals, or going to concerts, or turning on your sound system, or a radio or TV, why not try making your own music? Why not plan a regular evening when those who live with you, or your friends who spend time with you, know that this is to be the plan for the evening?

Who knows what new symphony might suddenly come forth? Or what new combination of instruments might suddenly be 'discovered' as a means of expression not *quite* like anything else!

For those who have this hidden longing for music in some form, but who have thrust it aside, there is another suggestion: the possibility of making a collection of musical things that would bring great satisfaction, and also provide a means for creativity. One could collect books on the history of music, or on the music of a variety of countries, folk music, unusual instruments and so forth. One could collect unusual string instruments, old clavichords or harpsichords – browsing around city second-hand stores, keeping an eye out for 'finds'. One could collect native drums or wooden wind instruments. Something might emerge in the area of *making* music because of such collections, or in giving lectures, or simply in acquiring satisfying knowledge and fulfilment.

There is really no need for a background of music school, or acceptance into a good orchestra as violinist, or public acclaim as a concert pianist, or even an invitation to play in church, in order to fulfil one's capacity in music. A woman who has married and is 'tied down', or a man who has had to dig ditches or be the president of a huge business firm, do not have to bury their musical talent under the bed, or shut it up in a box, and say – "Well, you know I am unfulfilled because . . ." or "You know I have a warped personality, that is I have psychological problems because you see I can't . . ." or "I'm so frustrated because 'it' is all locked up in here, I can't give expression to . . ." The talent, no matter how small and hidden, can be developed. You simply express yourself in music for your children, the children of the neighbourhood, your friends, or neighbours whose windows are open! – and for *yourself*. I have told in *L'Abri** how Jane came to a

* *L'Abri :* Norfolk Press, London and Tyndale House, Wheaton, Illinois.

place of certainty, after much prayer and struggle, that God was calling her out of opera, where she was having a tremendously successful career, into the work of the L'Abri Fellowship. She was willing simply to cook, garden, scrub floors, talk to people and teach the Bible. There is a place for the conscious sacrifice of the expression of a talent, asking God to show His will for the use of our lives in any way He plans – rather than insisting that it must be fulfilled in particular ways. It is a turning from or giving up – with complete trust that God really *is* love, and all wise, and would not waste the life of any one of His children.

There was a time when Jane did not even practise her scales, let alone sing in public. The 'corn [grain] of wheat' was really in the ground. But then came the willingness to use her voice in the most humble ways. That great operatic voice, trained, accustomed to singing to thousands, began to be used to sing with, and sometimes to, a group of cerebral palsy children on Sunday afternoons. This was not a prelude to something 'greater', but a willingness to use her talent to give joy to these children and lead them in worship, and in a way which was at the same time excellent therapy. After that she began to sing in our chapel, without an orchestra, and in our small L'Abri concerts. But other things began to develop, as a whole area of creativity in music began to grow and develop like a plant in good ground. I cannot help thinking of that musical career and talent which was 'planted' by being given up.

A new record has been made of music at L'Abri. On it are young people's voices – Shiro with his guitar, Sharon's clear, bell-like voice, Judy and others. Here is informal singing, music coming forth in sheer expression of joy, freedom and fulfilment, but captured in permanent form for people at great distances from L'Abri to share in. Gini's organ and piano playing, the spontaneous blending of voices among those who have met in L'Abri – people who have chosen to put aside ambitions, and are simply enjoying musical expression without the desire for 'success'. Jane's inspiration while listening to some of the beautiful things produced in this spontaneous way was to grab a tape recorder and get some of it taped. After much time and work on her part, this record has been produced, giving a new dimension to Jane's own fulfilment in music, and a new illustration of small sparks bringing forth fires, and the reverse – fires lighting the sparks!

Whether in music, or other things, one never knows what surprisingly satisfying things God has in His plan for the developed talent which is literally 'given' to Him to use or to lay aside.

For Christians there is a further point. The idea of making a "joyful noise unto the Lord" is expressed in the Bible. Singing, or playing an instrument in the deepest wood, on a lonely seashore, or on a wind-swept hill is not totally unheard. Birds might join in in reply, sheep might turn their heads, but this is not what I mean. There is a God who is there, and who is personal, and who accepts music as praise to Himself, as worship, when given to Him in this sincere way – without being strained through the 'strainer' of human acceptance.

If we followed the urging of God, as given through David in the Psalms, we would not be embarrassed to fulfil our urge to make music for God's ears alone. "O sing unto the Lord a new song; for he hath done marvellous things . . . The Lord hath made known his salvation . . . Make a joyful noise unto the Lord, all the earth: make a loud noise, and rejoice, and sing praise. Sing unto the Lord with the harp; with the harp and the voice of a psalm. With trumpets and sound of cornet make a joyful noise before the Lord, the King. Let the sea roar, and the fulness thereof; the world, and they that dwell therein. Let the floods clap their hands: let the hills be joyful together before the Lord . . ." There are also these words from the New Testament: "And be not drunk with wine, wherein is excess; but be filled with the Spirit; speaking to yourselves in psalms . . ., singing and making melody in your heart to the Lord . . ."

For Christians, there is no need for alcohol to release our inhibitions in music-making. The reality of the Holy Spirit should free us to joyous expression in the form of melody and song. This is what is meant to be *now*, and what will continue in eternity. Creative creatures on a finite level, made in the image of the Creative God.

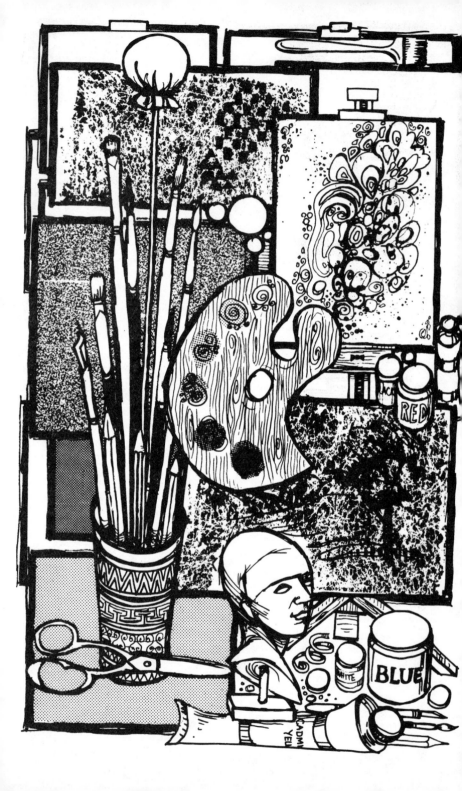

4. Painting, Sketching, Sculpturing

Do you have to be a great artist whose paintings are hung in the galleries to fulfil your talent for painting and sketching? Do you have to win a scholarship to an accepted Academy to fulfil a desire within your fingers to carve something out of wood, or form something in clay? Perhaps you have always longed to go to art school but had to take a secretarial course instead. Perhaps you graduated from a good art school but you got married soon afterwards and then the children came one after another. Or perhaps you are a man who has been torn between two careers. You wanted to be an artist and you have a talent for it, but you went into the family fuel business instead – and it is terribly crushing to be sending out tons of fuel and doing all the office work, while your art is lying buried! Or perhaps you have great longings to paint and sketch, but really very *little* talent, and you are embarrassed by the results of your attempts, so you never try it any more. Maybe you are a perfectionist who cannot accept his own work as satisfactory, so you stick to the science lab, and do no more art, beyond a few doodles on the phone book.

Everyone who has any talent at all in sketching, painting, sculpturing or carving, should have the opportunity to use that talent. The expression is important for the person, and can tremendously enrich the lives of other people. What can you do?

First of all, be satisfied with the fact that although your art or talent may never be accepted by the world as anything 'great', and may never be your career, it can be used to enrich your day by day life: enrich it for you, and for the people with whom you live. And secondly, come to a recognition of the fact that it is important for you to *be* creative in this area to the extent of your talent: important for you as a person who *is* a creative creature.

You paint murals on your kitchen walls, if you have that kind of a kitchen, and that much talent. I am visualizing a farm-house kitchen in Holland, full of shining brasses and copper kettles and antique furniture, with an amazing background of old Danish paintings, copied by a man who had enjoyed making these walls a work of art. You paint the walls of a child's room with panels of silhouetted deer leaping up the thin line of a mountain, or you experiment on the cement walls of a cellar playroom. You fix a bulletin board where you can display a different water colour or oil as you progress in ideas, or you use boards or old tiles as a medium for painting, and decide later how to fit the result in somewhere.

It is not necessary to attempt such ambitious projects, however. You are writing a letter to a friend, your fiancée, your husband or wife, your children . . . but as you express yourself or your mood better with a sketch than in words, you sketch at the top of the page, or intersperse writing with sketches. They can be beautiful, serious or amusing. You have made the letter more interesting and more communicative. But you have also enjoyed yourself and stimulated your own imagination in the doing of it. Ideas carried out stimulate more ideas.

You are a housewife with masses of things to get done in a day, or you work and then come back to an apartment or house, and have cooking and housekeeping to do in the evenings and on 'days off'. *Everyone* needs a list of 'Things to be Done Today' or 'Things to be Done before the End of the Month', or 'Things to be Finished before Summer'. There are shopping lists, lists of improvements to make in the house, lists to spur one on to more efficient living, lists including diet and exercise to lose unwanted weight, lists of letters that need to be written, lists of what to plant when in the garden. What could be a better outlet for a sketching talent than decorating such lists with artistic colourful or amusing sketches? Lists that are decorated with black and white sketches, or with a variety of coloured felt pens, come alive for you, and help to spur you on to do what is listed – to say nothing of becoming a decoration for your kitchen or office bulletin board. The same sort of thing can be done with lists handed to someone else ("Please get these things at the store on your way home", "Please plant this stuff in April", "Please remember *not* to eat the things listed here on your trip . . . remember what the doctor said", and so on). We are not all cartoon artists, but any flair in that direction can have a place in human relationships. Requests or demands are softened and take on importance when they are decorated with touches of beauty or humour. At the same time there is a fulfilment of that which is in danger of being destroyed by filling out endless tax forms.

You are having a dinner party, or it is your son's or husband's birthday, or your flat-mate passed her exam, or it is Valentine's Day, or you've been in the middle of a Los Angeles smog for a week – whether it is an occasion of celebration, a time of depression or dullness your talent for sketching can be used to make the dinner table more vivid with hand painted or sketched place cards appropriate to the occasion. Individual attention given to such moments and original ideas carried out can be an expression of love and care which cannot be duplicated by buying something 'ready made' or plastic. Perhaps your talent for sketching can be used in 'drawing' with icing on the cake for this occasion – more than just "Happy Birthday", but some sort of an appropriate picture, flowers or books. If it is a time for a card, do not simply buy a card (if you have hidden and unused artistic ability that is), but sketch one, paint one, or paint a whole booklet to commemorate a big occasion. While this is an outlet, it is also something which develops human relationships on a real and *human* level, rather than an artificial and plastic one. Anyone can sketch cards or little booklets in small areas of space, with materials carried along in a briefcase. This can be a good use for part of one's lunch hour at work, or for the interminable wait at the dentist or doctor's surgery (doctor's office, for Americans).

You are a housewife or cook, for whom the whole thing has become dull and prosy. You have to write out menus for special occasions – Christmas, New Year, Sunday High Tea – and also menus for every day, perhaps following a plan for a week ahead. As you write the menus, do not just scribble them on the back of an old envelope, but select art paper, or at least good quality paper, and embellish your menus with illustrations: table settings, food, garden scenes or market scenes, or just decorations. Do *something* more than simply write out the menu. Then pin it up where it will encourage you in your cooking, and encourage others who are hungry for a meal. It will not only be efficient, but will also add importance and dignity to the task of cooking. Your kitchen will take on a more interesting air. Perhaps it will not be a duplication of an art studio, but at least it will have a hint of something more than the peeling of potatoes.

Painting, Sketching, Sculpturing

Even if you cannot sculpt great fountains and statues, because you have not got that sort of talent, at least carve a child's toy, the head for a rocking horse, the handle of a wooden spoon, or make a figure to put in a miniature window garden. Start *somewhere*. Do not let this desire be simply a frustration that turns into bitterness when it could grow and develop, given some small outlet.

You teach a Sunday school class of children, or you lead a Scout group, or you give time to amusing children in a hospital ward, or you give a few weeks to camp work with underprivileged children, or you just gather some neighbourhood children for an afternoon, or you have a family of your own. There are times when games or songs can be illustrated with posters descriptive of the words. Try your ingenuity at making a different kind of an animal with an ear or a nose to be pinned on instead of the donkey's tail. Invent your own game which gives you scope for sketching or painting something you would enjoy doing. Illustrate songs with paintings, drawings on a blackboard, or sketches in an art book, and hold these up while the children sing. Prepare a tiny song book, illustrated, for each child. If your group is not too large, and you do just a few songs, you may develop it into something you will want to put in a more permanent form later. Do not wait until someone asks you to illustrate a book! The children will be thrilled with their hand-made books, and you will have enriched your own life, as well as theirs.

Recently my granddaughter Elizabee was coming out of church with her red loose-leaf notebook under her arm.

"What does your grandmother draw in that book during church?" she was asked. "May I see it? What is it all about?" The enquirer had seen me sitting between the two sisters, Elizabee and Becky, rapidly drawing all through the sermon.

"Well you see," answered Elizabee, "Becky and I don't understand Av's sermon, and Noni translates it for us." She is accustomed to hearing people translate the English that is preached into Spanish, German, or French for someone who cannot understand. My rapid illustrations and whispered explanations of the sermon, drawn while it is being preached, seemed a natural 'translation' to her.

Here is something which is a challenge to anyone who can draw at all, something I have done for years for my own children, and am now doing for another generation of children. A sermon can be 'illustrated' and thereby 'translated' at the same time, to a child sitting beside you, provided the child has any interest at all in understanding.

Let me give you a couple of examples. These are exactly as I took them down as the sermons were being preached, and of course are not a full report of my husband's outline, but are as much as it was possible to 'picture' during the preaching time – *not* worked out ahead, nor changed afterwards. I want you to have the exact original, so that you'll see that *you* can do it, too. I am not an artist as you see.

I might say that my husband's sermons are usually an hour to an hour and ten minutes long, which gives time for the development of the 'translation' as well as giving him time to present a full study. As I draw I whisper small explanations into the ear of the child, as well as writing, or printing some explanations. The printed explanation serves two purposes: first it means the child can go home and retell the sermon (with some help) to mother; second, it means that a collection of such sermons can be kept for years, and the re-reading of them brings back understanding and memories of the time when the shared hour took place. There is a value in continuity in life. There is a value in the 'remember when' sort of recollection. On top of all the other things to be gained by using your sketching talent to 'translate' sermons, lectures or stories for the children of your acquaintance, there is the additional gain of having been able to make a gift to memory.

Sunday October 23

For Elizabee and Becky ～ Sermon by F.A. Schaeffer
"The Active Obedience of Christ"

Behold
The
Lamb
of
God

John   Jesus

Paul Says —

ALL PEOPLE WHO ACCEPT CHRIST AS SAVIOUR ... (the white hearts show that these people have believed) **ARE SAINTS ..... WE ARE SAINTS .. NOT BECAUSE WE ARE GOOD BUT BECAUSE JESUS WAS GOOD .. FOR US** (IN OUR PLACE)

We will put BLACK ♥ HEARTS to show that people are sinners and do not believe God ...

White people have WICKED AND HEARTS

Black people have WICKED HEARTS

We will put WHITE ♡ HEARTS to show that people who believe God and accept Jesus as Saviour have their sins washed away

white people AND Black people Now have clean hearts

JESUS
ALWAYS WAS GOOD
NEVER SINNED

ALL PEOPLE

HAVE ♥ (SINNED)

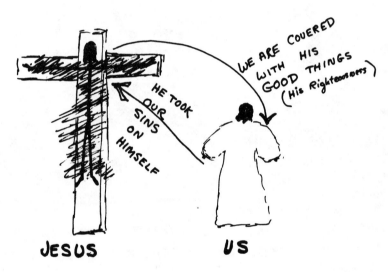

WE ARE COVERED
WITH HIS
GOOD THINGS
(His Righteousness)

HE TOOK
OUR
SINS
ON
HIMSELF

JESUS   US

When people know and
Believe then
they have ♥ (clean hearts
with sins
washed away)

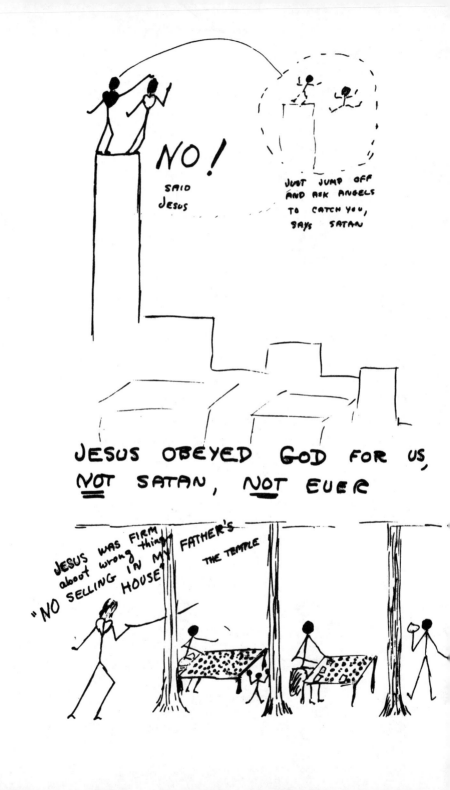

JESUS PREACHED TO THE
PEOPLE. ... BUT HE KNEW
THEY WERE HUNGRY SO
HE WAS KIND AND FED
THEM

THIS LITTLE
BOY GAVE
ALL HIS
LUNCH TO
JESUS, IT
WAS ALL
HE HAD.

JESUS TOOK THE BREAD
AND FISH AND PRAYED...AND
BECAUSE GOD CAN DO ANYTHING
HE MADE IT INTO ENOUGH TO
FEED ALL THOSE PEOPLE
AND THE BOY TOO...... AND THIS
MANY BASKETSFULL WERE LEFT OVER.

COUNT THEM!

JESUS IS THE GOOD SAMARITAN
HE WAS ALWAYS GOOD

JESUS OBEYED GOD THE FATHER
EVEN WHEN HE HAD TO DIE FOR
HE PRAYED " NOT MY WILL, BUT THING
...... WHATEVER YOU WANT ME TO DO
.... I WILL DO, OH GOD............

JESUS WASHED
THE DISCIPLE'S
FEET - - - - - -

HE CAN WASH
OUR SINS AWAY.

THIS LITTLE
BOY UNDERSTANDS
AND ACCEPTS
JESUS AS
HIS SAVIOUR

THE SAME
LITTLE BOY
IS NOW
COVERED WITH
CHRIST'S RIGHTEOUSNESS
(JESUS' GOODNESS)

AS IF WITH HIS DADDY'S COAT

ONE MAN DID NOT HAVE A
WEDDING GARMENT ...... !

JESUS WILL GIVE US A
WEDDING GARMENT.....

YES JESUS DIED
FOR US

BUT

HE ALSO LIVED FOR US

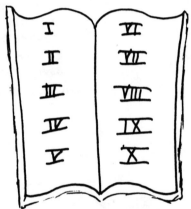

JESUS KEPT THE LAW FOR US
SO WE ARE SAINTS - - - - - ...
PRAY FOR HIS HELP TO LIVE LIKE
SAINTS -

Painting, Sketching, Sculpturing

I add a page overleaf from another day's Sunday sermon in Ashburnham to show that it is possible to portray, in some way, things which are often thought of as too abstract for a child. It is important to let children know that certain marks on paper represent something, but do not picture it. The three dots for the Triune God, for instance, are recognized time after time now by these children, and it is a quick and graphic way of letting them know you are talking about, or picturing, the Father, Son and Holy Spirit. Note the question, answered by "no" or "yes". Not only in church, but even when you are drawing a picture story to amuse a child, participation in what you are doing by posing a question with a simple yes or no answer, pencil held poised, waiting for the next chance to write, is a helpful means of holding wandering attention.

I would go on to say that if you are a Christian in communication with the living God, and you find you communicate better in drawing than in writing or speaking (and some people are like that), then sketching can have a place in your communication with God. If you think in pictures, and express yourself in drawing, it would be quite natural to take some of the promises of God and sketch them as you pray. You think of Jesus standing in a boat in a stormy sea and commanding the waves to be still. You sketch the stormy sea as you pray to the One who is able to still it, you write some of your deepest problems on the waves, picturing the fact that they are about to overwhelm you, and you bring them to God as things that only He can solve and can 'calm'. You sketch a boat, with a tiny figure of yourself (a stick will do) in the boat, and picture Jesus in the boat, too – remembering to thank God as you pray that He really is in the boat of daily life, in this stormy sea with you. If you are the sort of person who expresses himself in drawing with greater vividness, this can make prayer more vivid, and your communication more alive and real. It can have the effect of lifting it out of a stereotyped area of phrases.

EXCERPTS FROM a SERMON at ASHBURNHAM CONFERENCE BY F.A.S. "translated" FOR MARGARET and KIRSTY Sept.7

GENESIS 1 —

" IN THE BEGINNING GOD....."

● FATHER

● SON

● HOLY SPIRIT

(WE CANNOT
DRAW GOD..
SO WE WILL
USE THREE
DOTS TO REPRESENT
GOD)

BEFORE THE BEGINNING

Before anything else was........

God the Father

THERE WAS God the Son

God the Holy Spirit

I PETER 1:20

BEFORE THE BEGINNING

THERE WAS LOVE and COMMUNICATION

God the Father
Loved the Son
God the Son
Loved the
Father
The Holy Spirit
Loved the Son
the Son Loved
the Holy Spirit
the Holy Spirit
Loved the Father
God the Father
Loved the Holy Spirit

Did love
have a
beginning? NO

I Love You
LOVE
ALWAYS
WAS

Did Talking

AND hearing
have a beginning?
NO communication
ALWAYS
WAS

Did
the
world have
a
beginning?
YES

Did trees have
a beginning?
YES

Painting, Sketching, Sculpturing

I often sketch mountains, with prayer requests of the most 'impossible' kind (humanly speaking) on the peaks, remembering that He has promised that as we ask with faith – faith as a mustard seed – we may expect to see mountains cast into the sea. A tiny dot of a mustard seed is helpful to picture in contrast to the mountains. Prayer is communication with the God who really is personal, and who deals with us as persons. If sketching is your sort of communication, use it with other human beings, but remember that your communication with God is to be not *less* vivid than with men, but *more* vivid and real.

There is no need to lock up this capacity for expression because you have not been able to make a career of it. Develop it for your own sake, for the enrichment of the lives of those you live with, and as an unconscious spark to set fire to other dry wood, other creative creatures on a finite level.

5. Interior Decoration

We all live somewhere. A castle, a palace, a mansion hidden by
acres of wooded land, a large town house, a suburban home with
lovely gardens, a farm house set back from the road among rolling
fields, a cottage by a brook, a Swiss chalet in the Alps, a villa
above a lake, a modern home of old bridge timbers, rock and glass
fitted into cliffs overlooking the sea, a house identical to hundreds
of others in a housing area, a tiny house built against other tiny
houses with common walls between them – all in a row, or a flat
in a block of flats, an apartment in a New York skyscraper, a

trailer or caravan in a park full of these, a tent in the desert, a hut in the jungle, a bamboo house on stilts above water, a one-roomed tree house, a room in someone else's house, a stuffy room at the back of a boarding house, a one-room cave in the rocks, a thatched roof cottage with ceilings you can touch with your hand, a clearing in the woods where you can put your sleeping bag, a room in a hotel for ten days – *some* kind of a spot in the world is the place we each call '*home*', no matter how temporary that place might be.

I would put under the heading of 'Interior Decoration' anything we do with the place where we are living for any length of time at all. Here, wherever it is, is *your* spot. This place should be expressing something of yourself. It should be communicating something of *you* to your visitors, but it should also satisfy something within you. You should *feel* 'at home' here, because you have made it home with something of yourself.

It seems to me that, whether it is recognized or not, there is a terrific frustration which increases in intensity and harmfulness as time goes on, when people are always daydreaming of the kind of place in which they would like to live, yet never making the place where they *do* live into anything artistically satisfying to them. Always to dream of a cottage by a brook, while never doing anything original to the stuffy boarding-house room in a city; always to dream of a rock, glass and timber house on the cliffs above the sea, while never putting anything of yourself into the small village brick house; or to dream of what you could do with a hut in the jungle yet never to think of your inherited family mansion as anything but a place to mark time, is to waste creativity in this very basic area, and to hinder future creativity by not allowing it to grow and develop through use. Trying out all the ideas that come to you, within the limits of your present place, money, talents, materials and so forth, will not use up everything you want to save for the future, but will rather generate and develop more ideas.

So why not surround yourself now with things that communi-

cate something of your appreciation, your taste and your interests –
in wood, stone, glass, ceramics, crystal, pottery, china, textures,
fabrics, weaves; in colours, shapes, and sizes which please *you*?
Express yourself not only in selecting things to buy, not only in
your choice from many things displayed in a store, but also in
what you can produce yourself, with some degree of originality,
craftsmanship or artistic creativity. There is great satisfaction in
making something out of nothing, in restoring some old cast-off
to a place of usefulness and beauty, or rescuing some discarded
piece of wood, stone or metal from the dump and turning it into
an object that has purpose and charm in your home. Among other
things, this would also help to limit the ghastly filling up of dumps
and the wrecking of woods and fields with everything that people
toss out in order to make room for the latest plastic replacement.
Ecology is of vital importance in our moment of history. People
are worried about the imbalances man is producing in nature –
worried about what will happen in the future with the composition of seas, lakes, soil, and air. You are adding to the problem if
you are carelessly tossing out things which could be useful. On
top of that, you are neglecting to stimulate your own creative
talents if you throw away things and adopt an attitude of 'buying
whatever the local store might have'.

Remembering that we are finite, limited creatures, and that we
do not have the time or talent to do *everything* that will be
suggested, let us consider some practical possibilities.

Candle-making is almost a lost art. There is candle dipping,
and candle moulding. If you want to make a hobby of this, you
can buy materials – wax, moulds, wick – and books of instructions.
However, everyone has stubs of candles, though many people toss
them away as rubbish. These could be saved in a box, melted down
and made into candles again. If you have the professional equipment, stubs can be used for your moulds, but if not, it is possible
to use an empty tin can. You save the can after you rinse out the
tomato juice, dry it and start pouring in your wax (melted in

another tin can), combining colours in any way you like. To fasten the wick in the centre, stick it into the first half inch of wax when it starts to thicken, and tie the top end to a piece of wire fixed across the top of the can. Then pour in another inch or so of wax. You can get more professional instructions, but anyone can use an evening this way, with much satisfaction at the time, and pleasure in using the candles later. Floating candles can be made in small, shallow tins. White floating candles can be lit as they float in a bowl of water coloured blue with vegetable colouring. But you can think up your own effects!

Furniture can be designed and made by anyone with a talent in that direction. Some are very professional at cabinet making, others can do carpentry or upholstery or have a knack for restoring old wood. Others can make amazing things from cross-cuts of hard wood trees, tables with the bark forming a rim around the sides, chairs cut out of a log, fur or leather stretched across a frame, original designs of a tremendous variety of materials. Most of this takes a certain amount of money and talent, but *something* can be made for your home with a very little money and a very little talent.

Let me relate some instances from our own experiences. Fran and I were married in the summer between college and his starting theological seminary. It was at the time of the depression. We had no money, and jobs were not to be found. Our first summer was spent as counsellors at a summer camp on Lake Michigan. For the first six weeks during the girls' camp, Fran helped in the kitchen, lifting heavy pans, peeling potatoes and so forth, and I was given the job of 'life saving' during the swimming time. During the next six weeks as Fran became a counsellor for the boys' camp, I was given the job of teaching leathercraft. Now I had had no experience in leathercraft, but I devised a number of things to be made out of leather. We had punches for the boys to work with, scissors and leather. Ideas had to flow from what could be done with these three things. We had no prepared spools of thin strips to use for lacing, so circles had to be cut from leather. I found that as one cuts an eighth of an inch thin strip, and continues to cut round and round the circle (as the circle gets smaller, the strip gets longer) one can get very long strips of leather thong with which to lace a variety of things. We made belts, purses, wallets, book covers and so on – not tooled, because there was no equipment for that, but with a variety obtained through the diversity of leather.

Once a week we took a trip to a nearby leather factory, where we could buy scraps for twenty-five cents a pound. Some of the scraps were quite large, some were lovely strong cowhide, others were soft calfskin, some were coloured, others soft browns and beiges, and there were always pieces of startling white, and some of black. As I handled and chose pieces out of huge piles of scrap, ideas began to form in my head – ideas that came from the question "What are we going to do for furniture?" Our combined 'salary' for the whole summer consisted of board and room, and about $30 (about £9 at that time) plus payment for petrol (gasoline) for our model A Ford in which we had driven out from Philadelphia, and would drive back again. Out of wedding presents we had bought a sewing machine and a table. The rest of the furniture was still just a question mark. Fran had rooted through a dump and had come back with some marvellous finds during our last weeks of dating, just before we were married – so we had a collection of good springs from old couches and an old front seat of a car, among other things. All this was stored in my parents' home, along with some lovely pottery dishes I had collected by visiting the 'seconds' room of the Stangel Pottery factory during college days, and other like 'treasures'.

Now, during the summer, furniture literally began to take shape. We got a nailkeg in a hardware store – for nothing! We padded the top with some cotton and an old shirt, and stretched old material over the sides, to make it smooth. Then came the leather. One circle cut out of a strong tan cowhide covered the top. Then strips of the cowhide folded to follow the lines of the barrel staves were tacked on the sides so that they looked like one piece arranged in folds from the top down. A band of beige leather was tacked with tan upholsterer's tacks to form a band to cover the joins, both at the top of the barrel, and near the bottom. It really was a handsome stool! We saved the left-over scraps of that tan leather, and used it to make bands which were decorative and at the same time formed handles for the old chest of drawers we painted cream to match the old iron bed we also painted cream. The same leather covered a wastepaper basket, and formed bands on an old dressing table – and the maple wood mirror someone gave us as a wedding present was exactly the same colour as the leather. With a bedspread and curtains made of material which blended with the cream and brown, some copper candlesticks and so on, there was no feeling of 'make-shift' about it. Incidentally, that nailkeg *still* has the leather intact, and is still being sat upon thirty-five years later in our bedroom in Mélèzes. It has served its purpose as a stool, and crossed the ocean as a packing box for toys!

That same summer an old fashioned round cheese box turned into a white leather footstool, with brown and white strips laced together to form the sides. A damaged cowhide, which had been tossed into the pile of scrap leather, plus many rather large scraps of white and yellow leather, formed the cover for the strange couch Fran made out of the springs he had brought from the dump plus one half of a 'pull-out' day bed. It may not have been very comfortable, but that brown, white and yellow couch with its hand-laced stripes really did give an elegant effect.

When we came to Switzerland, not only was the wooden barrel which held our dishes made into a red leather covered chair, but all the packing boxes were turned into bookcases. These have lasted fifteen years and are still strong. So you see, making things out of 'nothing' can be more than a temporary makeshift.

Although antiques are so much in demand these days, and prices therefore tremendously high, it is still possible to find really lovely old things – tables, chairs, chests, desks and so on, in second hand stores or at auctions, and restore them yourself. I remember Fran taking chairs with him, one at a time, on pastoral calls out in the country around Grove City, Pennsylvania. He would sit outside near the barn where the farmer was working, or on a farm porch where the farmer's wife was knitting, quilting, or peeling apples, and talk to them while he sanded our chair. It did not detract from the conversation at all but added a feeling of sharing work as they worked. Whatever your life work may be, the re-doing of furniture – finding a beautiful grain under coats of paint, or bringing out grain that has been lost in varnish and dirt – is still a satisfying piece of creative work. I have found, by the way, that the best finish for furniture, once all the varnish is off, and the grain is clearly revealed and no longer dark with dirty streaks – is to give it an oil and turpentine treatment. One takes a glass jar or preserve bottle with a wide mouth, and puts a cup of turpentine in it, and a cup of linseed oil. Place rubber jar rings on the bottom of a pan of warm water, place the jar with the oil and turpentine in it on the jar rings (to keep direct heat from touching the glass), then place the pan on heat – a low gas flame, or low heat on the electric stove. As the water heats, the oil does too. The furniture (to obtain the best possible result) should be placed in warm sunshine, outdoors on the grass if possible, until the wood is warm to the touch. Naturally if one is going to work outdoors, the furniture should be in the sunshine long before one heats the oil! If you wish to darken the wood (I prefer to leave it the natural colour) this first coat is the one in which to add a dash of burnt sienna (oil paint) and a dash of vermilion or scarlet (if one wants a red-brown).

Take the hot oil and turpentine (with or without colour in it) and a soft old rag (someone's old cotton knit undershirt). Dip the rag in the oil mixture and wipe it generously on the furniture until every bit is covered with oil and turpentine. Now it is very important not to leave it on longer than ten minutes before you start to rub it, to get off all the excess oil. You must persevere until not a trace of extra oil can be felt. The warmth of the sun and the heat of the mixture causes it to soak in, so that, especially the first time, there is not much excess. This process is to be repeated seven times. Each time one should diminish the turpentine, and increase the oil – until the seventh time there should be no turpentine at all. The ideal length of time between coats is a week, although it is possible to do it with as little as three days in between. If there is sunshine each time so much the better, but if you should do it inside, be sure to warm the room where it is being done. Direct sunshine does have a better effect, however. The finish is one which is excellent for table tops: water does not leave spots, as it does on some varnishes. Each coat takes more rubbing, as with each coat the excess is more difficult to remove. Very fine sandpaper can be used in between coats also.

There is something very healthy about finishing furniture this way, restoring past beauty, rather than throwing it away and replacing it. It is rather like sitting in the grass of an old apple orchard munching a rare flavoured apple you selected from a tree yourself, compared with buying apples wrapped in purple-tinted, sprayed paper in a city supermarket. Doing something *yourself* will fulfil a need in you. And living with what you have made or restored will help you to express something which is you, living with an originality which speaks of the diversity of human personality as against the machine. Creativity is a part of personality. Surely the place where you as a personality live should speak of your creativity in some way!

It is possible to buy a weaving loom and learn to weave your own cloth. It is possible to have a wheel and a kiln and make your own pottery and ceramic works of art. It is possible to blow your own glass, make your own silver, scoop out your own wooden bowls, or weave your own baskets or chair seats. It is possible to cut squares out of all your old woollen clothing, or scraps left from sewing, and make your own woollen quilts. It is possible to cut strips and sew them together and braid your own rugs. It is possible to embroider your own tablecloths, or make needlepoint chair seats and backs. It is possible to knit your own lovely travelling rugs or couch covers, and it is possible to crochet your own tablemats. It is possible to make lamp shades and devise your own lamp bases out of bottles, old pitchers, or blocks of wood. It is possible to learn how to paper, paint and decorate a room entirely yourself, or cover the walls with jute or tapestry. It is possible to transform a room, or a houseful of rooms, without making huge structural changes, by making or blending together furniture in unusual ways – ways which your imagination 'creates'.

A Wendy House is a delightful English term for what Americans call a play house. A man who enjoys constructing a house, or who is a frustrated architect, a man with dreams of one day building a log cabin in the wilds with his own hands, or one who spends time drawing up plans of a dream building nestling in the curve of a hill or on the cliff above the sea coast, should be fulfilling his dreams and talents on a practical and possible 'small scale' right *now*. If such a man has children of his own, or knows children in his neighbourhood, or is an uncle or has adopted nieces or nephews – one of the best outlets for his stifled creative daydreams is *gathering* wood planks, logs, stone or brick, cement blocks or straw, whatever material is available and within the possibility of his bank account, and *planning* something around what exists at that particular moment! Now the drawing board and plans can have immediate execution! Now the clever ideas can have immediate praise, the excited and genuine praise of the best critics – happy children. A Wendy House or a play house can be simple or elaborate. It can be one room, or two or three. It can be a tree house, a log cabin, a little brick house, or a model of an African hut. Little boys would love a house with space for making things out of wood or clay – designed to be a workshop or a studio. Such a Wendy House could be made in an attic or cellar as well as out of doors. Little girls love to 'play house' and delight in a place to serve tea to friends, as well as to sew, paint or do creative things themselves. There are things to be learned, as well as things to be tested or demonstrated in building on a tiny scale. There is the combined fulfilment of creativity and making some other human beings very happy, as well as the probability of sparking off a fire of creativity in these other small human beings as they watch you work.

Of course you cannot do *every*thing. The list above is not meant to be followed completely. Of course we are limited by time, and by talents – but everyone can do something original, something creative, in the spot where they live.

Start somewhere. Do not walk into your home and be satisfied if there is no originality there, so that it looks as if it had come out of a department store, wrapped up in one piece, so to speak. Start where you can – perhaps with a children's nursery. Our daughter Susan has had ideas for Kirsty's nursery which are being enjoyed by the children who meet there for Sunday School. It is startling to realize that that play house used to be an old dining room sideboard. With the drawers removed, the door taken out and the struts removed which used to hold the drawers, the supports that the drawers used to run on have become tiny shelves for doll cups and saucers, doll candlesticks or tiny books. The whole thing has been painted and decorated with hand-painted flowers and designs in colourful profusion. Little curtains drawn back give the front opening the look of both door and windows at once. There is a panel on one wall of this room filled with Swiss calendar pictures, as though it were wall paper. "A child won't notice" is a very bad and untrue phrase to admit into your mind. A child *will* be affected by originality, beauty and creativity. And a child in a Christian home should connect being in communication with the Creator God with having been made creative, in His image. Rather than creativity being squashed out it should be enhanced and developed *because* of being brought up in a Christian home, *not* in spite of it!

Toys, of course, often need to be just toys. However, at times toys can be a part of the 'interior decoration' and still be enjoyed as toys. Home-made blocks of lovely polished wood of different grain, varied in colour, can be an addition to the beauty of a room, instead of a jarring note. Trains or trucks carved out of different woods are also an adornment to a room. The same is true of lovely wooden animals, or a doll's house that a creative father has made out of some good wood he found in the attic.

I remember the fun Fran and I had making a rocking horse for Susan. We simply could not afford anything that we liked, and her great desire at that age was for a rocking horse. Fran found some old broken furniture and used all the bits that were usable. He took the rockers from an old rocking chair, the seat from a child's high chair (and cut it smaller) and the legs from another chair. He fitted these legs into the seat (now cut to resemble a horse's back – proportionately at least) and then into the rocker. Then he carved a horse's head and neck out of a piece of mahogany we found in a barn. It had come from days when packing boxes were made out of mahogany, and was still lying around in a loft. Then my part came in! I took an electric needle and burned in eyes and some finishing touches on the head. I made a saddle out of an old leather brief case, worn at the edges, but still handsome in the middle. I put a piece of black fur on the head and down the back of the neck – which had an amazingly realistic effect – and then lined with red felt two pieces of the fur (real fur taken from an old coat) which had been cut into earshaped pieces. The felt made the ears stand up pertly and gave them a hint of realism in the partly seen, partly hidden red. Reins were made from an old belt, and the 'crowning' feature was a tail. When Fran made pastoral calls at places where people had horses, we asked for some of the horse hairs – ones that had fallen from the horses' tails! We spent one long evening spreading out the hairs individually, one by one, until they were all untangled, and then we glued, and I sewed, them together at one end and fastened them at the back of the seat behind the saddle. I must say it did look lovely by the fireplace, and Susan loved it more than any she had seen in a toy store. You can imagine the satisfaction of a combined creativity in this which could not be bought at any price.

Toys can be made not only out of wood, but also out of discarded pullovers and cardigans. When the mice ate holes out of my woollen things which were safely in a drawer one horrible November, my only consolation was the *Winnie-the-Pooh* animals which came out of what was left. Children are not the only ones who would like grey wool Eeyores, or little pink wool Piglets, or brown wool Poohs, or yellow wool with an embroidered stripe Tiggers!

Interior Decoration, as I intimated before, is *not* just one's artistic efforts, but is that which your home (even if it is just a room) *is*. If you are 'decorating' with clothes draped on every chair, with scratched or broken furniture – it is still your interior decoration! Your home expresses *you* to other people, and they cannot see or feel your daydreams of what you expect to make in that misty future, when all the circumstances are what you think they must be before you will find it worthwhile to start. You *have* started, whether you recognize that fact or not. We foolish mortals sometime live through years of not realizing how short life is, and that TODAY *is* our life. The day comes when we die. In some lives the day comes when one must live in an 'interior' about which one can do nothing. Take old age. There is an active old age for some people, like Ernest Shepard who did three hundred coloured illustrations for *Winnie-the-Pooh* in his English country home during his ninetieth year. However, there is another kind of old age which puts a person in a chair, not to walk or move alone at all. There is another kind of old age which limits a person by weakness, pain or illness to doing only the very basic things. Just as children need help before they can begin to decorate interiors or build houses, so old people need someone else to make their 'home' what they cannot make it. It is unfair to judge a person who is unable to move around by the 'home' they have surrounding them. Old people and disabled people should have thoughtful friends who spend enough time to discover their likes and dislikes as to colour, texture and so forth, and who would take time, thought, creative planning and money to *do* something practical about changing whatever is ugly, unattractive, or even just unfamiliar and unappealing to *that* personality. Changes could be new wallpaper or painted walls and woodwork, new curtains or a spread for the couch or bed, an arrangement of pictures, or something as simple as a new table cover and some plants. Ingenuity and creativity can be fulfilled in doing something for *other* people, for people in an old folks' home, as well as for people who are in their own homes but can *not* do the things they would like to do. Help someone else to have surroundings that express their likes and dislikes. Help some frustrated people to have a homelike atmosphere by fulfilling some of your own creative talents in a totally altruistic and unselfish manner.

Many of the examples I have given need a *house*, a more or less permanent home. What, you may be thinking, do you mean by 'expressing yourself' in a hotel room, for instance, or the back room of a boarding house?

I would say this. I often advise brides who are travelling during their first weeks or months of marriage to start 'homemaking' in a hotel, even if they are there for only a night, rather than groaning about having to "wait so long to have a home". How? Here are just a few small and simple ideas.

One may buy a small tablecloth, large enough for a table for two – a good one with the idea of using it throughout a lifetime. This can be spread on the table in a hotel room (hide the hotel cloth in a drawer) and used continually. It is surprising how that small thing can change the 'feeling', and make it *your* room. You could add to this a candlestick. Never travel without a fat candle that stands alone, *or* a candlestick, not too heavy a one, but one that you like – a silver one, for instance, or a small pewter one, or

a not too heavy brass one. Your own cloth, your own candlestick –
and then a flower: just one rose or one daffodil is enough to make
a difference, if you cannot afford more. If you are in a city, a
flower bought on the street; if you are near the woods or fields,
you can find some leaves, ivy, a piece of bark, some wild flowers,
a moss-covered stick; if near a beach you may find some smooth
stones or shells. You will be surprised how much difference it
makes to have done *something* to make a room your home, even
for one night. If you are travelling for a length of time, or are in a
'temporary situation', it is important to have things which will
last. Continuity is important. To have familiar things around us is
to feel 'at home'.

I am not saying that continuity of familiar objects is more
important than the central and most important continuity of the
Christian fact – that we are citizens of a heavenly country, that we
look forward to a home which is being prepared by God, which
will be a creation of the all-perfect Creator, and which He has
promised will be more marvellous and beautiful than we can
possibly imagine. Of course we have a hope that is a comfort to
us, and of course He has a purpose for us now which has central
importance, and of course the suffering involved in this present
life, fulfilling this present purpose of His for our life, is not to be
compared with the wonder, glory and beauty of all that is ahead
for us. And of course we are to be willing to sacrifice in the area of
material things as well as in all other areas, to put first the things
of God, to put first His use of our time, our money and our
talents.

But all this does not erase the fact that as human beings made
in the image of God we have all the marks of personality. We are
not machines. We have sensitivity and creativity in some measure
and in the midst of carrying out the purpose God has for us – in
the midst of sacrifice of time, money, luxury and self-indulgence,
in the midst of putting God first and someone else second and self
last – we can still have the fulfilments which help us to be balanced

and whole creatures, rather than torn, lonely, unbalanced, splintered people. As human beings we do respond in certain ways to certain *things* as well as to other personalities, and God.

Think a moment of the things God has surrounded us with – blue spruce trees, weeping willows by a lake, tiny paths under huge arches of entwined branches, ponds thick with water lilies, cascading waterfalls with spray catching the sunlight, geraniums red against thick green leaves, stretches of wheat and corn fields as far as the eye can see, orderly rows of vegetables bright in a spring rain, falling brown leaves forming a carpet underfoot, the first snowdrops bursting forth as the spring snow is melting, violets and moss at the edge of the woods, seeds spread out on your table which you can sow and visualize the growth ahead. God has surrounded us with 'things' which give continuity to life. We feel 'at home'. We can have emotions of satisfaction, quietness, familiarity, *continuity*, when we scuffle through the leaves at fifty-five in exactly the way we loved to do when we were five; or when we watch and count the waves breaking with every seventh one coming in with a greater splash – at seventy, just as we did when we were seven. God provides us in this life with a continuity in the universe which we may live with as we watch the Milky Way, as well as promising the wonder of all that is ahead for all eternity.

Consider a child. Anyone who knows anything about travelling with children, or taking children from one city to another in a big move, or from one country to another in an emotionally disturbing 'change', knows that it is important to take along the 'lovey blanket' without which the child has never gone to sleep, and the most beloved and familiar toys which spell 'home' to that particular child. A tiny baby travels more happily and without as much shock and disturbance if he sleeps in the same carricot or folding crib as he slept in at home, and a wise parent who knows that changes are ahead starts the baby sleeping in something which can be taken along, so that psychologically the change is not so much of a disturbance.

Interior Decoration

As adults we should not ignore the fact that we too respond to familiar things in some measure. It is stupid to try to be 'hard', 'brave' or 'stoical' about that emotion called 'homesickness' or 'lostness'. A continuity which can help in the midst of tremendous upheavals in life is a continuity of things with which one is surrounded, even small things.

It seems to me that some of the frustration of not being married, on the part of some men and women, is caused not only by the lack of sexual fulfilment, but also by the lack of any sense of making a 'home' with a continuity of *things*, right now. You dream of the kind of interior decoration you would choose to use as a background for your dreamed-of 'home' which is a far off *future* thing involving an imaginary person. Stop dreaming! Make the place where you *live* a place where you are expressing your own taste right now. But also start collecting some things which will continue to be used throughout life, and will be *your* familiar 'things' that will give you continuity.

A single man or woman can have a collection of silver spoons, or a favourite tea set, or a small painting, a lovely tray, a fine bed cover, an antique oil lamp or an ancient set of candlesticks – some things that, barring disaster, can go with you wherever you go, from one house to another, from one city to another, from one country to another, from one job to another. These few things can go in a suitcase, but they will be your familiar surroundings, making the next place – hut or palace, tent or mansion, have a continuity for you. If these are things you have made in some way, then so much the *better* for the continuity and the fulfilment, transforming a new unfamiliar place into a home which has ties with the past.

If you stop putting off 'homemaking' until your hope of marriage develops into a reality, and start to develop an interesting home right now, it seems to me two things will happen: first, you will develop into the person you could be, as you surround yourself with things that express your own taste and ideas; and second, as you relax and become interested in areas of creativity, you will develop into a more interesting person to be with, and other people will very likely find that they will enjoy being with you more!

Surely each person who lives in an 'interior' of any sort should realize that 'Interior Decoration' is the first opportunity to bring forth 'Hidden Art', in some small measure. And for the Christian who is consciously in communication with the Creator, surely his home should reflect something of the artistry, the beauty and order of the One whom he is representing, and in whose image he has been made!

6. Gardens and Gardening

Almost anyone can have enough soil, light and seeds to become involved in the magic of growing things. Everyone recognizes that there is creativity and artistic talent involved in Landscape Architecture, but one does not need to have a degree, nor even a tremendous talent, to enjoy and bring enjoyment to others through the medium of gardening. God's planted garden was both pleasant to look at and its produce was good to eat! There should be something of both these aspects in every person's garden. I am not threatening the careers of landscape gardeners or landscape architects by urging everyone to attempt expression in this area of 'Hidden Art'. It need not be much to be enriching to your life. It need not even take a lot of time or study in order to express something to which other people can respond or provide something of the healing of getting your fingers into soil – the very opposite of the machine or the plastic life of the city.

You may have 300 acres to work with, or three; a large and fertile garden surrounding a suburban home, or a tiny square space in the back of your city home; you may have a large balcony with space for oblong or round boxes or containers of some sort, or only a windowsill or two. Whatever it is, there is something very basic in being involved with a growing, living art form such as a garden of some sort. One can grow flowers, vines, small trees in pots or barrels, vegetables in beautiful rows and lush variety; one can have a full herb garden surrounded by its own little hedge, or a miniature herb garden in a window box. There is something very exciting about holding tiny brown seeds in one's hand, in rubbing soil in one's fingers to make it fine in texture, in putting some natural manure at the right depth to give richness to the soil, in placing the seeds with one's own fingers in the rows, in covering them up and patting them. There is something exciting in watering the bare brown ground, wondering whether the hidden seeds are doing anything at all, wondering whether they will burst out of the little shell and become roots going down and stem and leaves coming up. The day the first tips of green are seen, if they are *your* seeds, planted by your own fingers, there is a thrill that is surely similar to producing an art work, a thrill of accomplishment mixed with the reality of what *is*, what *exists*, what the universe consists of.

Human beings were made to interact with growing things, not to be born, live, and die in the midst of concrete set in the middle of polluted air! Growing plants are supposed to be doing something to the air human beings are breathing, and human beings are supposed to be doing something to the plants. It seems to me that to remove *all* direct contact with soil, seeds, plants, trees, flowers, fruit and grain is as devastating to normal, balanced, fulfilled human growth as removing all direct contact with a home with its natural interaction among human beings of different ages. People throw away natural fufilments which would give them necessary outlets as well as development as personalities, and then rush to psychiatrists. Far better to spend some time in developing a variety of the hidden arts for which you have some talent, including some which take you 'back to the soil'. There is something tremendously fresh and healthy in having one's mind filled with thoughts of whether the lettuce is up yet, whether the pea pods have begun to form, whether the tomato flowers are being pushed off by the tiny green fruit yet,˙and whether that Crimson Glory rose has any rival in fragrance in anyone else's garden.

Men who know, men who have been studying and doing research, are becoming alarmed about the destruction of the original balance between soil, plants, animals, air; water, plants, insects, fish and air: showing so clearly that man – the human race – rather than interacting with and carefully caring for the things God created to be in relationship with him, to give him environment and atmosphere, and opportunity not only for staying alive but also enjoying fulfilment of all his talents and sensitivities – has in fact done the very opposite and has very effectively been ruining his own domain. To look at it honestly and frankly, what man has been doing has been tearing to shreds not only his 'home' but his food, his air, his beauty, and subsequently his own psychological makeup, in effect – *himself*. It is creativity and artistic production in reverse. Man the artist, upside down!

Ecology is a subject everyone is now discussing in a worried sort of frenzy. But it is one thing to sit around talking about how the balance of nature is being upset and how black the future looks because of this, to sit and discuss the tragic felling of age old trees, the hacking of chunks out of majestic mountains so that unspoiled beauty is becoming rapidly a thing of past memory; it is quite another to ask ourselves what we are doing about our own plot of ground, whether it is a little four by four foot square, or an acre, or a whole farm or forest. This is where we should be expressing some ecology in a practical fashion, where we should be doing some original landscape architecture which combines art with preservation and conservation, which produces a growing beauty, and which inspires other 'artists' to do the same thing.

A Christian, who realizes he has been made in the image of the Creator and is therefore meant to be creative on a finite level, should certainly have *more* understanding of his responsibility to treat God's creation with sensitivity, and should develop his talents to do something to beautify his little spot on the world's surface. Neighbours, friends and strangers walking by ought to find the Christians' gardens, farms, estates, schools, hospitals, huts, missions and factories, surrounded by beauty of grass, moss, rocks, fern, bushes, trees, flowers and vegetables, planted and cared for with an expression of originality and artistic planning on some scale. A Christian individual or organization should not move into a property and turn it into a shambles. The opposite should be true. It should grow and blossom into a place of beauty, demonstrating something of the wonder of the One who made plant life to produce seeds in the first place.

Christians should have *more* beautiful gardens, should be *more* careful to build without cutting down the lovely trees, should be *more* sensitive about keeping the brook unspoiled as it bubbles through their lands. Sadly, this has often not been so. Is it a waste of time to bring forth this sort of beauty, or to fulfil your artistic talents in this sort of way? Is it more important to use that time talking about the living God? It seems to me the beauty which causes strangers passing by to stop and *enjoy* a garden, provides a background and already 'says something' which gives an emphasis to what it is important to say. Of course one *must* speak of the historic and prophetic facts which people need to hear, the truth about God and the universe. But this makes much more sense in a setting which shows that action on the basis of truth really *does* fit in with the universe as it is, and was created. Certainly we who have a logical base for beauty, as well as morals, should be the ones to be fitting our landscape gardening into artistically beautiful and ecologically 'sound' treatment of land and plants.

On the route to Aigle from Ollon, where we live in Switzerland, one passes an orchard. Neatly planted rows of trees are beautifully pruned and trained to form straight aisles for fruit picking, with a

grassy carpet beneath. But the thing which causes most passers-by to turn and look, and look again, slowing up the car if they are driving, is the touch of an artist indeed. Planted at the end of every row of trees is a lovely rose bush, and in mid summer these bushes are a riot of colour in a variety of roses. There is just one rose bush at the end of each line, but this is enough to lift the entire work, which could be merely efficient fruit farming, into a work of art, enjoyed by hundreds who pass each day – bringing an influence into lives as well as being a subject of discussion, and bringing about, in other gardens, results of which the 'artist' may never know.

Gardens and Gardening

The first 'garden' Fran and I ever had was a wooden butter bucket, wide and low, filled with lovely black soil Fran had carefully gathered from a forest, and given a layer of manure to enrich it further (down in the middle somewhere). During those depression days after college, as he attended seminary, we were living in a downtown Philadelphia apartment – top floor rear of an old row house. We had a tin roof, surrounded by an ugly barrier, on which to step out and hang up our clothes. The wooden butter tub was the source of a transformed view! We could not substitute trees or mountains for rooftops, brick walls, electric wires,

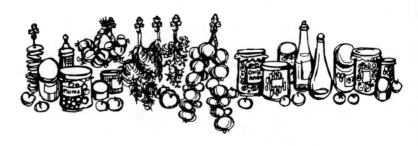

telephone poles and rubbish cans in bare dirt yards, but we could improve the immediate view of a tin roof with that ugly wooden barrier. We put the bucket in the middle, right by the barrier. At the back we planted heavenly blue morning glories. Oh, the excitement of their actually coming up, and starting to climb the hopeful grocery string carefully tied in position for the start of their climb! And oh, the greater thrill when they began twisting themselves beyond the strings up to the barrier . . . and made their way across the top, in both directions! We put dark blue-purple and white petunias next, then some blue ageratum in front of those, and finally ivy and green and white striped leafy vines at the front to spill over and down to the tin. When the morning glories bloomed we used to count the number each breakfast time: "27 today . . .". "This morning it's 29, can you believe it?" Those amazing heavenly blue morning glories produce new blooms each morning which die at the end of the day – and ever more blooms the next morning.

It really was fantastic to see the difference made by the vine covered barrier and the flowers spilling out and over on to the tin roof. I felt as if I had a rather elegant penthouse – especially by the third summer of our marriage when Priscilla was born, and I sat out there rocking her carriage to put her to sleep in our 'garden' surrounded by the heavenly blue morning glories, for all the world as if we had a cottage in the country! The whole thing gave a satisfaction that cannot be described, a feeling of elegance. It surrounded us with flowers and atmosphere, gave us something to water, weed and watch grow, fulfilled something in us and made the surroundings bearable. It had an effect on other people, too, and became a 'conversation piece', a place to start, with people who lived in the same building, or who came to see us.

The first vegetable garden came when we finished seminary and went to our first church, in Grove City Pennsylvania. There we had a rambling 'back garden' that was next door to a garage on one side, and a filling station on the other. However, for a combination of reasons, we wanted a vegetable garden. Many of the people in our congregation had gardens. People in small towns grew their own vegetables in those days (as many still do, I'm sure) and we wanted to fit into the life of the people among whom we worked. But also we needed the help such a garden would be to our food budget.

However, it turned out to be a means of fulfilling our need for expression, and we were the ones who benefited the most.

Planting a vegetable garden can truly be an artistic expression. Rows can be planned from an aesthetic viewpoint, as well as a horticultural one. Tall and short plants, shades of green, corn and tomatoes with their form, texture and colours can be arranged to create a total artistic effect. Poring over seed catalogues in the winter can be a thing of aesthetic anticipation and creative planning, as well as a mouth-watering experience.

So with our garden. Digging the weedy grass into a brown oblong patch of soft soil was hard work but excellent exercise. Planning and planting a colour and texture scheme was fun, and really exciting when the plants began to come up in amazingly straight rows. The contrast of dark soil and green shoots made early weeding something like erasing pencil marks from a watercolour. Finally we discovered that the result of Fran's having put double the normal amount of manure was a fantastic crop of tomatoes – enough from three rows to have plenty to eat raw as long as they lasted, and to 'put up' twenty-two shining quart jars full for the winter. This was satisfaction indeed.

I remember some of the gardens of the farmers in our congregation, their tables spread with food that they had grown themselves: strawberries picked from rows of straw mulched vines – the straw keeping the deep green leaves from ever being muddy, let alone the berries. These were things of beauty as they grew, as they were picked, and as they were served: shining rows of raspberry jam on loaded shelves, beside rows of perfectly shaped peach halves waiting for winter Sunday night guests; rows of vegetable soups made from marvellously fresh vegetables picked and prepared by the children; apples in bushel baskets – yellow, red, green – the varieties painting the cool fruit cellar like a canvas in a museum. Art. '*Hidden* Art'. Some of the farmers and gardeners of history have blended the variety of their tasks into a similar and satisfying expression of 'Hidden Art'.

Oh, the frustration and the monotony of not being able to be creative because of feeling that there is no time to pursue any of 'the arts', and that one must simply do the 'office work', or whatever is our daily work, and collapse at the end of the day! A change can be as restful as any other kind of rest, and a change which gives fulfilment to otherwise hidden and suppressed creativity can do even more than 'rest' in releasing frustration.

Gardens and Gardening

Gardens in L'Abri are a part of the therapeutic kind of activity which gives not only outdoor and earthy work, but some creative opportunity as well. Studying the intellectual and philosophical answers to the questions of life and the Bible is more meaningful when undertaken in a situation involving such activities as digging, planting, weeding, picking, caring for chickens, sawing wood, making shelves and furniture, cooking, sewing, painting walls, and so on. Gardening, among other forms of creativity and hidden art, is something which can be a shared activity. Not only can the

important techniques of gardening be taught to the new gardener as he works with an experienced one, but there are spiritual lessons to be learned – *examples* in the garden that cannot be learned so vividly anywhere else.

"I am the Vine, ye are the branches", says Jesus – and when one works with vines having branches the practical reality brings the words alive. "He that abideth in me, and I in him, the same bringeth forth much fruit: for without me ye can do nothing."

"Except a corn of wheat fall into the ground and die, it abideth alone." One sits on the ground with a grain of wheat or with a kernel of corn and thinks of this as one pushes it into the ground, gets dirt in one's fingernails in the process, and pats it with the palm of the hand. "But if it die, it bringeth forth much fruit." Is it going to rot there, watered and buried, out of sight in the darkness – dead, in such a real sense? Dig it up and see the discouraging 'first appearances' after a day or so – but wait, watch – with water and warmth of sun, with the life within ready to burst, suddenly the first sprouts appear, and you can watch day by day, week by week and begin really to feel the reality of what Jesus said as that one grain multiplies itself. "He that loveth his life shall lose it; and he that loseth his life for my sake shall find it." One sighs as one gradually realizes that there is simplicity here, and great and complicated depth all at one time. To come to a place where one is really wanting to 'die' to self and ambition, to come to a place of seeming to 'lose' one's life by handing it over to God's plan is, it seems to me, more vivid for a person living in the setting of the seed-plant-fruit process, rather than always in the midst of the mechanical machine processes.

The parable of the sower comes to life: "And some fell among thorns; and the thorns sprang up with it, and choked it . . ." Oh, the weeds! You can weed and weed and weed, and if you are away for a few days the weeds return to choke out the plants completely.

A double thing is happening, the understanding that 'art' in any form demands discipline and hard work; and the realization that in life there really are weeds in many forms which grow far more easily than the plants. The deep satisfaction of seeing the picture, painted not with oils but with the living mobile of leaf, bud, flower and fruit, is heightened constantly for the Christian by seeing the demonstration of the aptness of the biblical illustrations of Christian life.

This is all a part of man living in the midst of that with which he was created to interact. One of the greatest destructions in the whole field of ecology is the dehumanizing of man as he lives with machines, instead of with living, growing, responding plant and animal life. I am not advocating that everyone should rush off and become a farmer, or that we all should take a tract of land in Canada and be homesteaders, though that might be a very good thing! Rather I am trying to say simply this: whoever you are and wherever you live, take at least one small step now against the tide of destruction of the balances in nature, against the waves of plastic, and do something positive in the area of landscape architecture right *now* – even if only in a buttertub!

7. Flower Arrangements

Japanese artists make a life long study of flower arrangements, expressing their philosophy in this medium as well as producing works of art. It can take hours to make a Japanese flower arrangement, if it is done with precise attention to detail. Colour, texture, exact length of stem and degree of angle must be taken into consideration. It can be most complicated and depends on much study and understanding of all that is meant to be involved. This is an art that needs to be learned, an art which needs a teacher as well as talent.

However, anyone can express himself with some degree of originality in the area of flower arrangement. Every home can have something of this art form in it. Every spot where anyone lives can have something in the form of a "flower arrangement" which is not a permanent part of the interior decoration, not a life-long treasure to be taken from home to home, but a constantly changing source of beauty, a continually fresh 'finishing touch' to the surroundings. Here the one responsible for the homemaking (whether it be a wife or a husband, the shifting responsibility of one member of a group sharing an apartment, the housekeeper in a boys' boarding school, the cook at a camp, the nanny bringing up someone else's children, the single person living alone, anyone, except perhaps a prisoner in gaol – and *including* him if I were the matron of the prison!) has the opportunity to develop in this art form, to fulfil inward needs for expression, and to spring surprises of beauty which cheer up everyone involved.

In Holland fresh cut flowers are generally considered a necessity. We are told that even the very poor people in Holland put aside a guilder or two for flowers every week. Dutch homes are characterized by enormously wide windows at the front. As you walk down a street in Holland you are very conscious of flowers – flowers from front to back, in the rooms and beyond in the gardens. When someone comes for dinner, or to spend the day, or to celebrate a birthday or greet a visitor from a far country, whatever the occasion, if you are Dutch, you come with a handful of flowers, bought in the stalls beside the canals, in the town square, or in a florist shop. When I am in Holland I often remember the daily admonition recited to us in the Newburgh Free Academy in New York State where I lived when my father was pastor there during my high school years. Dr. Doughty, the principal, always started the daily assembly by reciting, "If you have two loaves of bread, sell one and buy a lily!" The students often used to giggle or smirk, or make sarcastic little whispers in reply, but it is not a bad idea! The bread becomes a different thing when eaten at a table with the lily in the centre.

I feel very strongly that this modern fear of the home becoming non-existent can be countered only if those of us who want to be sure our little spot is really a home take very practical measures to be sure that it *is* just that, and not a collection of furniture sitting in some sort of enclosure being protected from wind and storm. Of course, human relationships make a house into a home: either the relationships within the house, or the welcome and understanding that guests find. Human relationships depend upon communication.

But this communication takes time. It is also helped by atmosphere, and the atmosphere is helped by the 'things' which are arranged with love and with an expression of creativity in a visible form. One of the least time-consuming forms of artistic expression, as well as one of the most effective ways of making a table come alive, is to make an 'arrangement' as a centrepiece. There is a 'togetherness' at the table which comes into focus when all eyes are drawn to the centre. There is a tendency to talk about the beauty seen there, or at least to be affected by it. Some form of centrepiece, and some candlelight (if it is evening, a rainy day or foggy, then candlelight is the only good substitute for sunshine!) are invaluable in drawing a table full of people together to share food, thoughts, ideas and problems.

Does your mind immediately go to a table full of guests? This may be included, but it is not what I am talking about. I am not thinking of Christmas, or a birthday, or Sunday, or a special group of people whom you want to impress. A tired or discouraged husband comes home, a restless and frustrated teenager comes to dinner, fretful or squabbling children come in from play, the two year old is put up in his high chair, your room-mate comes in after an exam, friends who share a flat or apartment throw their coats on their beds. When the call comes, "Dinner is ready", "Supper is served", or "Hurry, the soup will be cold" then there should be something to bring realization, a warmth of knowing that someone has taken thought and put some originality into preparing the

place where food and conversation are going to be shared. It really does do something which cannot be achieved otherwise.

This is the day of the 'TV frozen dinner', stuck in an oven, served on a tray in front of the TV set, no conversation, no blessing being said, no Person being thanked, because there is no-one in the universe to thank. It is the day of 'grabbing a bite' and going on to the next engagement. The art of living together, of being a family, is being lost, just as the wealth of the earth is being lost by man's carelessness in his ignoring the need for conservation of forests, lakes and seas. The 'conservation' of family life does not consist of sticking a rose in the middle of the table; it is a deeper thing than that. However, whether one is sketching a face, building a house, designing a dress or planting a forest, one has to start *somewhere*. And in this need to get back to 'gracious living', to real communication among people living together, it seems to me one place to start could be the meal-time moments, and the careful preparation of the background for conversations at that time. Of course one gorgeously original and fantastically set table is not going to knit a scattered family together. But I really believe there is both an art form and a way of life, an atmosphere and a form of showing consideration, as well as a subtle way of providing education and inspiration in artistic areas that is being lost altogether if the meal table always has a bare centre – or a bottle of milk and a jar of pickles!

I am not necessarily advocating that you go out and buy a book on flower arrangements, and carefully try to buy all the bits and pieces, along with the flowers, to carry out its instructions. Some may want to take this up seriously as a hobby, or a new and concentrated form of art expression; and some may have money to spend on bowls, vases and flowers. Others would find this both discouraging and impossible. Anyway, the elaborate arrangement of flowers in a magnificent pottery bowl, shown in the book, might be completely incongruous in your home.

What I am talking about is something anyone could do, anywhere: an expression of individuality, personality, originality. Everyone has a table where they eat, either alone, or with others. That table can be made a pleasant place day by day, and at times it can be a breath-takingly beautiful surprise, or amusingly original. The decoration does not have to be the same thing all the time; and it does not have to be flowers at all.

Flower Arrangements

If you live by the seashore, you could collect shells and smooth stones and make an arrangement of them on a wooden tray or on the sand-coloured tablecloth itself. You could put among them two fat shell-coloured candles, or sea-blue ones. You could use a star-fish shell another day, in a pile of sand on a blue plate, and match a candle arrangement using three slender tapers placed in

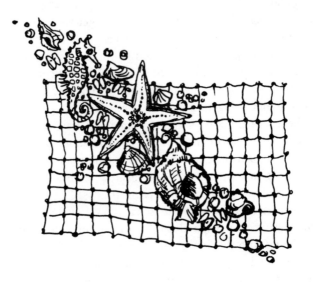

holders hidden under shells or pebbles from the beach. If you live near the woods, or walk in woods occasionally, you could collect different varieties of moss. This could be used to cover part of a small twisted branch fixed in a wooden bowl, in which a single flower in a concealed container appears to be growing by the log. Moss can be used to cover violet or mayflower roots, so that they seem to be growing in the moss. A log can be placed directly on a tablecloth of brown or dark green, and long pieces of ivy twisted around it, with two candles in their brass holders set in the places which look best to you. As an alternative, cover a rock with some of the moss, put it in a shallow container that holds some water, and float a chrysanthemum, dahlia, short-stemmed open rose, or any large flower on the water – with moss on the rock, and some covering the container, you have the effect of a hidden spot in a stream somewhere.

If there are small children in your home, make a 'garden' with moss on a tray, and 'plant' little flowers in it, placing small twigs for trees, and whatever else you find that will give the effect of a miniature garden. Sprinkling this with water will make it last a few days, but it is to be thought of as temporary, of course!

If you live by fields of straw, wheat and grasses, you could arrange a vase of wheat – or even put it directly on the tablecloth. Or you could dig up a plant (geranium, begonia or African violet) and 'plant' it on one end of a platter, with some leaves or ivy covering the rest, returning the plant to its place in the garden or flower pot later on. You can use leaves, ferns, spring twigs in bud or autumn leaves in colour, arranging them by sticking them in flower holders, placing them on the cloth, or using them in vases. You can keep your eyes open for holly of interesting shapes and textures, dried weeds or thistles with lovely bleached creamy-beige tones, and keep your eyes open for candles (or make your own) to blend in with the rest of your 'decor'.

"This cabbage is too beautiful to cut. Isn't it just like a gigantic green rose?" Have you ever said that? So why not put it on a silver platter, in a crystal bowl or on the tablecloth itself, and let everyone enjoy its crisp and beautifully shaped leaves tonight . . . then eat it tomorrow! Or you could make an arrangement of a lovely stalk of fresh Fordhook celery, two or three green and yellow peppers, a cucumber, some smooth, perfect onions, and a stalk of corn. It is worth thinking of this as you go to the market – picking some things for the centre of the table, to be used one day that way, and eaten the next. Keep all these arrangements flanked by candlelight. It is possible to grow gourds in your garden, just to have the shapes for table arrangements. Perfect shaped mush-rooms are also a surprising addition to a vegetable arrangement.

Fruit, of course, can be used it other times. And, for children, try scooping a hole in an apple just the right size to hold a yellow or red candle. (Cut a tiny bit off the bottom to make it steady when it stands.)

I grew pale, green gourd-shaped squash (marrow in England) in our garden one summer, just to use them for Sunday High Tea table arrangements. The leaves wilted fairly quickly, so I left arranging it until the last minute. When the sandwiches were prepared, I rushed out to pick a few of the lovely shaped squash leaves and then arranged them with some of the orange flowers and pale green or green and white squash, with tendrils of the vine curling round. It made a kind of oval shape, streaking out from one corner of the long coffee table, with tall white candles in brass candlesticks completing the arrangement, and open-faced cucumber sandwiches (with a dot of mayonnaise and a sprig of parsley on each one) blending in with the colour of it all. In spite of wilting leaves after a period of time, the memory of that table is as vivid as if it had been painted on canvas. Indeed, the memory of even short-lived beauty makes it worthwhile to take time and energy to provide a background of beauty for the human relationships developing in your home.

Children growing up in an atmosphere where beauty is considered an important part of daily life cannot help being inspired to develop their own original ideas in these areas, nor can they help being prepared to live aesthetically themselves. There is a 'togetherness' in sharing a prepared table that even very small children feel, although they cannot express it verbally. Instead of saying, "Oh it doesn't matter, it's only the children", when you are alone with children for a meal, it is important to say the opposite to yourself. "I wonder what the children would enjoy the most? Being surprised by something special on the table – a mirror with that new toy duck on it, and some stones around the edge, so that it looks like a pond, lighted by candles in crystal candlesticks, or pewter candlesticks . . . something that will look like lamps near the pond? Or would they rather have a choice, since they are the ones to be considered tonight . . . shall we have the green cloth, or the pink with pink candles?" It can be something that takes very little time indeed, but when the children are alone, do not let that be the moment to sit down at a bare table, or not to bother sitting down at all. Even the little one in the high chair will like to smell a single rose and look at it for a few minutes. (Of course, he may pull it apart or throw it on the floor, but through learning what to do with a flower, real appreciation grows.) Imagination not only provides a background of beauty to daily life, but also a realization that love, thought and preparation has been given to that 'together' time of eating.

People who are sick or in pain, whether in bed upstairs or in hospital, appreciate the beauty of flower arrangements more than anyone. Of course, they do get bouquets of flowers, but too often there are drawbacks: many, many flowers come all at once, too many to enjoy properly, at the moment when someone has had an operation, a new baby, a critical illness or an accident. Then for weeks, or maybe months or years, no one sends even a blade of grass! The people caring for the patient settle in to a routine, taking in the meal trays with an air of it being all they can do to get there with it, plopping it down in all its bareness, and walking out. Secondly, when flowers do come they are often not arranged with any kind of thought, and are placed where they can have no relationship with the person, and form no 'centre' at all for any gathering around the bed, nor are they close enough to the person to be the kind of 'communication' they could be. Why not try sending *one* rose in a lovely pottery vinegar bottle with a slim neck and a handle, or a dahlia floating in a crystal bowl for the hospital patient's tray? Then continue sending one flower a week.

Whether you are caring for someone during long periods of illness, or for short times of convalescence, imagination can be employed in preparing the meal trays. A candle on the tray brings light, warmth and aliveness of movement into the drabness of being shut away not only with the illness, but also with the disappointment of not being able to do whatever it was that would have been done otherwise. A flower in an egg cup or a tiny vase, or just a piece of ivy or a few coloured leaves or fern, placed at one corner of the tray – any bit of decoration will lift the meal tray completely out of the category of sheer utility. It will become a human experience of being cared for, rather than of being pushed aside.

But trays that are arranged with originality and beauty (special tray cloths, special napkins, grass mats, tiny tea-pots, individual china made especially for one-person-meal-on-a-tray) should not be thought of as something only for the sick. You have a child, or two, who are fussy and you know they are tired. Instead of a squabbling, scolding supper-time which will make things difficult for everyone involved, try sometime saying, "I have a surprise for you, a bubble bath (or some other special bath ingredient), and then a surprise tray in bed, let's hurry!" It isn't any harder to set a tray or two with a tiny bit of decoration – the bread and butter given a quick shape with raisin eyes, or some special touch. The relaxation of a bath, the surprise interest and fun in the tray with its decoration, makes the simplest of food a treat, and is apt to make going to bed fun, instead of a punishment. This can be preceded or accompanied with reading or talking together.

You cannot expect to have a close relationship with a teenager who, after all, is still the same person as the two-year-old you stuck crying into bed, the three-year-old you spanked and shoved aside, the four-year-old you wouldn't listen to, the five-year-old you never shared beauty with, the six-year-old you found boring, or you 'trained' never to butt in, but never gave time to make a cosy and beautiful background out of which you could talk to him or her.

Whether it is a man and woman relationship, a parent and child, two friends, a nurse and patient – great moments of trust and confidence do not spring out of concrete. They need a long time of being planted, fertilized, weeded, watered, warmed by sun and cared for lovingly before they become mature 'plants' – plants of understanding communication and loving relationship. If you never have time to enhance moments together by making some preparation for beauty as well as for meeting necessities you are apt to miss altogether the spontaneous response and opening up of the personality which this would bring. An atmosphere of love and consideration, in which one is trying to anticipate the mood of others, requires something tangible, something that can be seen, as well as a feeling inside oneself. Expression which is felt and understood is not just conveyed in words, but in words accompanied by actions. You may feel I am giving the 'Hidden Art' of flower arrangement too large a significance but I feel that the 'caring' for others in the family, whatever that 'family' consists of, can be expressed over and over again in ways which bring a very warm chain of memories, through transforming an ordinary meal-table into a place of surprise and beauty.

I believe strongly that the suppressing of hidden artistic talents or appreciation has the effect of warping us as personalities. So I feel that this beautifying of meal tables and trays with hidden artistic and original ideas is a very simple area indeed in which to start fulfilling one's own needs, through the fredom of expression, and adding another dimension to the day.

Some may be feeling that all of this does not apply to them, because they live alone. But when you live and eat alone, it is most important to give thought to your own need not to feel neglected and lonely. Then, more than ever, you should be sure to get yourself the earliest pussy willows, the first daffodils (or your favourite spring flowers), and arrange them in a way which satisfies *you*, but with variety, finding new ways to do it from time to time. All the ideas I have given can be just as easily done by you for your table, your window sill, or even your stump in the middle of the tent!

I have been staying in a small apartment alone some of the

time while I have been writing this book. I have not wanted to take time for meals. But when I have stopped for a cup of tea, a glass of milk or a light snack, I find that it makes a tremendous difference if I arrange the dishes I enjoy, on the tea trolley, for instance, with a candle to light while I treat myself to being served in bed and read as I relax. The warm colour, glow and movement of the candle somehow dispels the 'aloneness'. It becomes a positive opportunity to read, pray and be quiet, and not merely a cold, shut-away, negative sort of thing. A fire leaping in a fireplace, the noise of crackling logs burning, the ticking of a Neuchatel clock with its shiny brass pendulum moving with exact precision, music filling the room as an orchestra or a solo violin burst the silence and scatter it into oblivion, achieve the same sort of thing.

I feel there is something special about preparing the background even for reading alone, or thinking alone, while one is eating a meal. Even aloneness can be a 'cared for' aloneness, instead of a 'neglected' aloneness. People talk of 'neglecting' themselves, and they think of not taking baths or having new clothing or washing their hair, or not taking vitamins or the medicine the doctor ordered, or of not resting enough or taking enough exercise. But I think there is another kind of neglecting oneself for the people who live alone – that of never treating oneself to a lovely flower arrangement and candles for dinner, or never giving oneself a meal in bed with a beautifully decorated tray, or never putting ivy and a violet plant on the stump one eats on in the field. There is a dignity gained in 'loving' oneself (we are to love our neighbours *as ourselves*) in the proper way. There is a psychological need met in surrounding oneself with beauty in the right way. There is expression that can be fulfilling even if other eyes do not see it and other voices do not say "Thank you".

For the Christian, aloneness is never alone aloneness in any case. One is always with God, always in the presence of God the Father as one's Father, and prayer is conversation with Him. One is in the presence of Jesus, who is our Friend, our Saviour, our 'Bridegroom'. And one has within oneself the presence of the Holy Spirit. Beauty is important to God. Beauty was important in the Tabernacle in the wilderness, in the Old Testament days. Beauty was ordered by God as He gave the plans to Moses. Beauty was given by God to Adam and Eve as a background for their walks in the cool of the evening. Beauty was created by God in the first place. It is not therefore unfitting for you who live alone to prepare a beautiful spot in which to eat, alone *with the Lord*; even as He has prepared the very flowers with which you surround yourself or prepare the table where you will sit and eat and talk with Him. You are created in the image of the Creator! If you have been afraid that your love of beautiful flowers and the flickering flame of the candle is somehow less spiritual than living in starkness and ugliness, remember that He who created you to be creative gave you the things with which to make beauty and gave you the sensitivity to appreciate and respond to His creation. Creativity is His gift to you and the 'raw materials' to be put together in various ways are His gift to you as well.

The Chinese women used to have their feet bound. Small toeless feet were supposed to be a thing of beauty, and a proof that the woman had never had to work in the fields. Country girls who had to work hard had unbound, free feet but the women who were aristocratic or wealthy had to hobble around or be carried, on feet that had had the toes bound underneath to prevent growth; little-girl feet that were painfully kept from being the lovely free things feet were made to be in the first place. It is a horrible thought, purposely destroying, by breaking and binding up, the feet that could otherwise have walked, run, jumped, danced, skipped and hopped. But some Christians have 'bound up' their various forms of creativity, and have needlessly crippled their personalities from running, walking and skipping.

This has nothing to do with willingness to sacrifice. I am not talking about luxury. This has nothing to do with wanting 'things' rather than wanting God's will in one's life. One can be led by God to live in a miserable slum in the heart of a teeming city, but one's little spot there can have some sort of beauty of leaf, flower, rock, branch and candle, whether there is a table or an orange crate upon which to arrange it. Even a mud hut can have ivy growing over it, and a flower arrangement within it on the flat stone, or the sawn-off plank which serves as a table. The people in the slum, the people in the other mud huts are not going to be estranged from beauty. Washing-machines or big cars may produce jealousy or envy on the part of those who cannot have them. If God puts you in the midst of people with whom He wants you to communicate, it is important not to have a huge gap materially between those people and you. There is no specific kind of house you must live in to be 'spiritual' – only the house the Lord has chosen for His chosen purpose for *you*, and the house with you in it. But whether it be a palace or a tree house, beauty is *important*, and this very simple form of producing beauty is really one of the most universally possible expressions of 'Hidden Art'.

I must add one more sentence to this chapter: please *try* something in this area today. The only way to start, is to start.

8. Food

Food concerns everyone to some degree. Everyone eats something, and everyone eats at intervals during the twenty-four hours that make up the time in a day. Vast books have been written about the nutritional requirements of the body and theories differ as to the best way to meet them. One could spend a long time talking about balanced diets, food essential to health and energy, food which helps to keep one young in looks and vitality, food which prevents certain body deficiencies, food which heightens one's resistance to disease, and so forth.

God who created us, created us to need food, and he created the food that we need. But He did more, much more, than that. Let me illustrate.

When the children of Israel were in the wilderness in the days of Moses, God provided them with a food that came down as snow. It dropped on the ground overnight and was good food for one day at a time. This 'manna' must have been a perfectly balanced food, with all the nutrients in it necessary to the human system. But the Israelites, instead of appreciating it, began to be hungry for the leeks, garlic and meat that they had enjoyed in Egypt. In spite of the fact that their nutritional needs were being met, that food was being provided without any work being involved and that they were witnessing a miracle, the people began to complain loudly. They were hungry for *other flavours and textures* of food.

This was wrong not because it is wrong to enjoy a variety of flavours, but because God had promised them that marvellous things lay ahead – marvellous food, among other things (milk, honey and grapes were mentioned) – and they did not really believe that this was true. They did not look forward with faith and trust in what God had promised, nor did they appreciate His way of caring for them at the present moment, nor did they have any patience. Their complaining was an indication of a lack of trust that the manna was temporary, and a lack of appreciation of the fact that it was a marvellous food while travelling to that which lay ahead, but was not meant to be permanent.

God could have created all food as a bland mixture of proper nutrients: something like wheat-germ, yoghurt and honey in a cake form, or some sort of fruit which would have contained everything necessary to good health. However pleasant the mild flavour might be, we cannot imagine eating just one single flavour all the time, the reason being that we have been created with taste buds, a delicate sense of smell, and a sensitive appreciation of and response to texture and colour. God has not given us sensitivities and appreciations which cannot be fulfilled anywhere in the universe He has created. In His perfect economy of creation God did not create loose ends. God made man with tremendous diversity in many areas, including the area of enjoyment of food. To meet this diversity, God made a tremendous variety or diversity of kinds of food.

It is worth pausing to remind ourselves of the variety of food God created, variety in colour, texture, flavour, smell and shape: the fruits, the vegetables, the sea foods, the meat, the grain, honey made by bees in rocks and trees, trees that give maple syrup and cane that gives sugar – what diversity! There is the smoothness of avocado and banana, the grainy feel of a large strawberry before you bite into the sharpness of flavour, the crispness of a water melon as your teeth break into the red firmness, the contrasting crispness of celery, lettuce and a pear. There is the variety of flavours and shapes in nuts alone: peanuts, walnuts, cashews, pecans and brazil nuts; and berries: blue-berries, raspberries, currants and blackberries. The variety of staple foods of various countries can be imagined by our taste buds, as well as in our mind's eye, as we think of fields blowing in the wind: wheat, rye, barley, rice, corn, and the thick flat leaves of potato plants covering huge squares of land. There are the colour contrasts and varieties: deep orange of carrots and the brilliant green of peas, the deep red of beets, and the sunny yellow of corn on the cob, the pale green of lima beans, the green and white of cucumber, the red, yellow and orange of tomatoes and peppers, and the purple of the egg plant.

Who made the pink salmon, the white crab meat, the fragrant odour of roasting lamb, and the flavour of charcoal-cooked steak? Not only did God create all this – but Jesus actually broiled fish over coals on the seashore, cooking it for breakfast with the disciples. He ate simple suppers with fishermen and wedding feasts with many guests. He ate a home meal with Mary and Martha, and the menu which the 'publicans and sinners' prepared. In the light of this, does it seem logical that God would be better pleased if we ignored food altogether, and ate only with the motive of taking necessary nourishment into our bodies out of necessity, rather than to fulfil any kind of aesthetic as well as physical hunger? The Bible says that God created things for us to "enjoy richly" and although sin has spoiled so much that complete enjoyment is now impossible, yet He means us to know something of pleasure and appreciation in responding to what He had made for us to have and enjoy now, as well as to have some realization that He, as designer and creator of all this, is well able to fulfil His promises to prepare something far more wonderful in that unspoiled eternity which lies ahead for those who believe in His Son.

Of course we must retain a balance in the use of time, money,

energy and priorities. There will be times when it is more important to continue a serious conversation than interrupt the flow and
communication to prepare an elaborate meal. There are going to
be times during our lives when we put aside preparing and serving
meals at all to continue in an important conversation for six, seven
or ten hours at a time. There are going to be days in the life of
any Christian who really communicates seriously with God, when
one puts aside food altogether to fast and spend unbroken, un-
disturbed time with Him. Reading the Bible, praying, writing and
outlining one's thoughts in prayer, sketching to illustrate prayer,
and spending unbroken time shut away in a room, or in the woods
or fields in a growing closeness to God the Father; giving oneself
to the help of the Holy Spirit in interceding for others; being
conscious of Jesus interceding for us – at such times one appreciates being separated from the interruption of food and conversation around meal tables. This will take place in the lives of
Christians at moments of crisis when decisions need to be made
and God's guidance is being sought – and at moments when for a
variety of reasons a day of fasting and prayer is in order. But, as a
regular, normal part of life, we are not asked to deny ourselves
food and the beauty, variety and originality of God's creation in
this area is to be enjoyed, not rejected.

Therefore cooking as an art – 'Hidden Art', if you want to call
it so – should be recognized and then developed in everyone who
has to cook, wants to cook, or could cook! Cooking should not be
thought of as a drudgery, but as an art. Talent in this art form
differs, of course, and would not be identical in each individual
even if developed, but that is not the same thing as not recognizing
it as an art form and not attempting to develop it.

The danger today, for both men and women cooks, is to take
the short cut of using prepared and frozen foods all the time,
using things from packages, bottles, tins and cans, rather than
starting with fresh food, or food from one's own garden. I am not
advocating that we never use anything pre-prepared, to save time

for other things, and I realize that many – perhaps most – people do not have a garden; but one can at least try to get away from the 'plastic trend' in the area of cooking and it is healthy, in several meanings of that word, to try to do so. Why not try to make your own bread and rolls once in a while – even once a week? It is possible to have a greater variety if you become proficient in bread making: variety of the basic dough from week to week (adding toasted wheat germ, oatmeal, soya flour, honey, brown sugar, more or less eggs, etc.); but also it is amazing how many things can be made from the basic dough.

We make dough at L'Abri on Saturdays, enough to feed a hundred or more people, and then form poppy seed rolls, twisted rolls with sesame seeds, and braided rolls with caraway seeds. These are used for hot dogs, hamburgers, or tuna fish salads. We take the same dough and make sticky buns full of lovely fat raisins, or orange rolls* or apple dumplings. Or we prepare sweet bread for Sunday tea by kneading in raisins, cut up citron and candied orange peel, chopped walnuts and a packet of candied

* Roll out a rectangle and spread on it a mixture of butter, grated orange rind and sugar. Roll up and cut off inch-long pieces. Placed in buttered muffin tins, let rise double, and bake.

cherries. This we form into a long loaf, cut it in three pieces and twist each piece until it is longer, then braid and place it on a buttered pan for rising and baking.

In the summer time we take the same dough and form oblong pieces about an inch and a half wide by about five or six inches long. These we put in oblong pans, well buttered, which have sides about two inches high. On top of each oblong piece we push in slices of fresh apricot, in orderly fashion, about five or six slices to each roll. Next each apricot-topped roll is further 'topped' with a mixture of brown sugar, butter, a tiny bit of flour, and ground nuts. Again one lets the rolls rise for a period, and bakes.

The variety one can obtain with home-made dough is as great as one's imagination. My suggestions give only a small idea, but an incentive, I hope, to commence.

Just as it is good to get one's fingers into the soil and plant seeds, so it is good to get one's fingers and fists into bread dough to knead and punch it. There is something very positive in being involved in the creativity which is so basic to life itself. Home-made bread, home-made cakes and pies, home-made vegetable soup from home-grown vegetables or from vegetable market purchases, home-made jams and jellies, home-made relishes and pickles – these are almost lost arts in many homes. For growing children at play, there is nothing so interesting as really 'doing things'. To 'help cook' is one of the most enjoyable things of childhood – to say nothing of being a sure way of producing good cooks. A child can cut up carrots at a very early age, with no more risk of injury than from falling down outside at play! A child can mix and stir, knead the dough and be given a piece to make a roll man, cat or rabbit with raisin eyes. A child can fry eggs or make scrambled eggs – one of mine did every morning from the age of three! The kitchen should be an interesting room in which communication takes place between child and mother and also among adults. It should be interesting in the same way as is an artist's studio, as well as being a cosy spot in which to have a cup of tea while something is being watched or stirred, or while waiting to take something out of the oven.

Food should be chosen for nutritive values, of course, but also to give variety and interest to meals. Food should be chosen to give pleasure, and to cheer up people after a hard day's work, to comfort them when they feel down for some reason, to amuse them when things seem a bit dull, or to open up conversation when they feel silent and uncommunicative. It seems to me totally unnecessary for any home, or even institution, to fall into the rut of serving the same thing the same day each week. One should not be able to say, "Oh, yes, Monday, bread pudding"–*anywhere*. Meals should be a surprise, and should show imagination.

Perhaps part of the reason why some people dislike cooking, or find meal preparation a bore, is that they get into a rut where menus are concerned. Variety makes food more interesting to cook, as well as to serve and eat. I have cooked for an increasing number of people for an increasing number of years, and I must say that it is not necessary to put aside variety because there are too many people. Indeed it is the other way around. It would become unbearable to cook for so many for so long if there were not the challenge of variety and the interest of making sudden last minute changes as the mood strikes, or if circumstances, such as an influx of guests, make it necessary. Chicken for six people can become enough for twelve if you cut it off the bones and make it into a Chinese meal by adding onions, peppers, almonds and pineapple wedges. Or it can just be cut into large pieces and put into the gravy to serve over hot biscuits–which themselves can be made when the influx of people is discovered to be coming in the front door. Making food 'stretch' can be a challenge, as well as a necessity. It is not necessary to have a large food budget to make meals interesting. In fact it is often the other way around. The need to 'stretch' the money often gives birth to ideas in cooking and serving.

It seems to me that in a world of starvation Christians should recognize their responsibility to share in a practical way with those who go short. So it is important for everyone, no matter how well-off they may be, to be careful not to waste food. There are two ways to avoid waste: first, one plans meals which balance the more extravagant ones with inexpensive ones; and secondly one uses left-overs – even the tiniest bit of left-over. Bones can be boiled to make broth, bits of vegetable can be used in soups or casseroles. Meat can be used for Chinese fried rice, soup, scalloped potatoes with ham or corned beef, in macaroni dishes, curry and so forth. To toss out food and buy new is akin to tossing out good furniture or fabric to buy new. This too is a practical side of ecology.

I know one cannot directly help the starving Third World by using the left-over stewed tomato in tomorrow's meat loaf, but it is really true that one saves money by cooking this way, and the saved money can be given to some project in either doing something personally for someone or in giving it to an organization. As children of God who will some day stand before Him to be shown the 'treasure in heaven' or the absolute zero in the heavenly bank account, the *waste* will be realized – it seems to me – by remembering, or being shown, what could have been done with what was wasted, as well as what should have been done with that which was spent with personal extravagance.

It is not necessary to have an extravagant food budget in order to serve things with variety and tastefully cooked. It is not necessary to have expensive food on the plates before they can enter the dining room as things of beauty in colour and texture. Food should be served with real care as to the colour and texture on the plates, as well as with imaginative taste. This is where artistic talent and aesthetic expression and fulfilment come in.

A man does not have to be the greatest chef in the world in order to enjoy the artistic fulfilment of cooking and serving a meal. A woman does not have to have a certificate from the Cordon Bleu or a Home Economics degree in order to develop both skill and creativity in planning menus and serving well cooked meals. For both male and female cooks, the variety within any one meal should be thought of. Eye appeal as well as taste appeal should be remembered. For those cooking for a hundred people, the beauty of each plate should be considered just as much as it should be for the person cooking for two. A plate can be thought of at times as a kind of 'still life' – not a lasting one, of course, but lasting in memory. Dishes should be a part of the background for the colours of the food, and as one chooses dishes there should be some variety – even if the dishes are polished pieces of wood, shells, or large leaves from the jungle! Naturally every meal will not be equally beautiful as a 'still life', because there are the masterpieces which only come once in a while – but the effort should be there, the 'mentality', as the French call it, seeing a plate of food as a thing of beauty. Not only does this give interest, atmosphere and pleasure to the meal, but it gives dignity and fulfilment to the one who prepared it.

Still life? A brown baked potato scored with a criss-cross cut and the fluffy white insides pinched up with butter and parsley on it; or sour cream and chives, sitting beside a red baked stuffed tomato.* Perhaps an ear of bright yellow corn is placed across the centre of the plate to divide the hot baked things from a crisp green salad and strips of bacon (or thin slices of cold meat or ham). Or how about shredded carrots with chopped nuts and bits of pineapple to make an orange mound on a green lettuce leaf?

Another lettuce leaf may nest two halves of an egg (either devilled, or simply cut in half in natural yellow and white perfection). Finely chopped green or white cabbage mixed with finely chopped apples and oranges share one or another of the lettuce leaves and bright green parsley sprigs top off the colour scheme, while a slice of cheese adds to the protein content, even if not

* Scoop out centre of tomato, leaving about ⅛ in. to ¼ in. thickness under the skin; mix with soft white bread crumbs, sugar, salt, black pepper; refill tomatoes and dot with butter. Bake until bubbling – about ½ hour.

adding much colour. Potato chips, hot muffins or scones could be added if you wanted something more on the plate, or could be passed around in a basket.

These are summer-time meals. Each season brings its own possibilities of special treats, of beauty, as well as of content and flavour. Broccoli which is fresh and picked at just the right moment of perfection provides a splendid green colour, as well as a tender texture and fine flavour to place beside meat loaf or a slice of roast and a mound of white mashed potato. A few radishes, tossed salad with tomato, or pickled beets can be added to this plate to give it the dash of red it needs. Those who live where sweet potatoes grow can add that warm colour to the greens and reds of vegetables that flank a slice of pink ham, or finish off a beautiful fish plate.

There is no occasion when meals should become totally un-important. Meals can be very small indeed, very inexpensive, short times taken in the midst of a big push of work, but they should be always more than *just* food. Relaxation, communication and a measure of beauty and pleasure should be part of even the shortest of meal breaks. Of course you celebrate special occasions – successes of various members of the family, birthdays, good news, answered prayer, happy moments – with special attention to meal preparation and serving. But we should be just as careful to make the meal interesting and appealing when the day is grey, and the news is disappointing. Children feel the difference in the home that takes this attitude. Father comes home tired and dis-couraged after some sort of failure or disappointment to find, not the food he dislikes, nor burned soup and sloppy serving, but a beautifully set table, with his favourite food served artistically, and a hot drink and some tiny cookies (biscuits) or nuts served afterwards with all the air of a special occasion. The room-mate receives a letter which is the dreaded reality of a fear long worried about, but comes back to the flat to find a meal prepared in anti-cipation, and the comfort of hot broth and melba toast, omelette and muffins, and chocolate scalding hot, topped off by a marsh-mallow or whipped cream. Food cannot take care of spiritual, psychological and emotional problems, but the feeling of being loved and cared for, the actual comfort of the beauty and flavour of food, the increase of blood sugar and physical well-being, help one to go on during the next hours better equipped to meet the problems.

If the one who cooks is the wife in a family, her attitude toward the marriage as a whole should be to think of it as a career. Being challenged by what a difference her cooking and her way of serving is going to make in the family life gives a woman an opportunity to approach this with the feeling of painting a picture or writing a symphony. To blend together a family group, to help human beings of five, ten, fifteen and sixty years of age to live in communication with each other and to develop into a 'family unit' with constantly growing appreciation of each other and of the 'unit' by really working at it, in many different areas, but among others in the area of food preparation, is to do that which surely can compare with blending oils in a painting or writing notes for a symphony. The cook in the home has opportunity to be doing something very real in the area of making good human relationships.

There are times when one cannot 'cook', when one is travelling and staying in hotels or *pensions*. It is much less expensive to buy food in grocery stores, meat shops, and markets, and to prepare and serve it in the hotel room, or wherever you are staying, than to eat in a restaurant. It is quite a challenge to see how many menus you can work out which do not need cooking, but which give variety over a period of time. All you need is cold, clean water to wash fruit and vegetables, some sort of a table, paper plates, napkins or clean paper on which to serve and paper cups or glasses. A cooked chicken can be cut into four or six portions, and be supplemented by well-washed lettuce, a tomato, a cucumber cut in strips and some potato chips (crisps). Rolls and butter and an apple for dessert can be added, with milk as the beverage. For another meal one can have a slice of cooked ham, carrots cut in long fingers, well washed celery, and radishes, with a bit of escarole or lettuce. Cream cheese balls with a nut stuck in them can dress up the plate, and brown bread and butter can fill you up! A sandwich meal can be made with cream cheese and nut with lettuce for one sandwich, and tomato, cheddar cheese and lettuce for another. Frozen orange juice with water added is a lovely fresh drink that can be made anywhere you can get drinking water. Bananas are an ideal dessert with this.

Fran and I have had some delicious uncooked meals, with endless variety, during our travels in various places. Our family vacations always had such uncooked meals on the beach or in the woods, and the children delighted in finding that no two days needed to be exactly the same. It is an amusing challenge, as well as money saving, and more interesting in the end. 'Tea' – the English and European custom of a four o'clock time of refreshment – was always more satisfying when prepared with a small electric coil for heating the water in a cup or jug, and an array of food prepared in the room. Rolls or buns bought at a nearby bakery, or left over from breakfast, can be cut into slices and spread with peanut butter, jam, a meat spread or cheese, to make small tea sandwiches which are really better than *patisseries*. Picnics prepared at home and taken to some outdoor place to eat come into this same category but have the advantage, of course, of the home kitchen for preparation.

Food and meal-times shared have always been thought of as a closer kind of communication than simply talking to people, without eating together. The very sharing of a short break to drink a cup of tea, a glass of juice or a cup of coffee together, is in itself a kind of communication.

The refusal to eat with another person at the same table is the negative of this. Some people – even some Christians – refuse to eat with someone of another colour, language, tribe or nation. This is strange, because the Bible says that in heaven some from every tribe and nation and kindred and tongue will be there. So we shall be sitting down at the 'Lamb's Supper' – the "marriage supper of the Lamb" spoken of in prophetic passages of the Bible – with some from *every* tribe, nation, kindred and tongue. That is God's demonstration of the reality of the oneness of man. This oneness can be seen only on the basis of what 'the Lamb' has done, because it is the Lamb of God – a name for Christ, who offered himself like a lamb for sacrifice – who makes it possible for men to be united in a real way. Just as the lambs were slaughtered in the Jewish temple to take away sin, so Jesus Christ offered Himself on the cross to take away sin and remove the barriers that separate man from God, and men from each other. And the oneness He creates will not just last the length of a single banquet, but for ever.

But Christ does not ask us to wait until that future day to eat with Him. He gives a promise, conditioned by man's response, to 'any man': "Behold, I stand at the door, and knock: if any man hear my voice, and open the door, I will come in to him, and will sup with him, and he with me." Fantastic! Christ says that He will come in and sit down at our table, whether it is the table of someone eating alone, or a table crowded with people. He – Jesus – will come in and sup with anyone who "hears his voice" and "opens the door". You do not 'hear' someone whom you declare does not exist, and you do not open the door to someone you are rejecting. But if we hear, and open, He will come in. I do not believe this is simply a picture of salvation. I believe that there is a very real sense in which Jesus will share meals with us, as He shared meals with Martha and Mary, or with the disciples on the seashore, or with great crowds of people, or with Zacchaeus, the tiny man who had climbed a tree to see Jesus. It is a promise of a communication which is very close and special. It also emphasizes to us the fact that eating in an atmosphere of communication is important to the Lord. Even as the edelweiss which grows unseen by human eyes beside some distant mountain rock, or the violet under a fern at the edge of the wood, is unappreciated by any human being because it remains unseen, yet still has purpose because the living God sees and appreciates each blade of grass and each flower as well as every sparrow; so the lovingly prepared meal which may not seem to find any response or appreciation from any human being is being shared by *Him* in a very real way.

Jesus said: "For I was an hungered, and ye gave me meat: I was thirsty, and ye gave me drink: I was a stranger, and ye took me in: . . . Lord, when saw we thee an hungered, and fed thee? or thirsty, and gave thee drink? When saw we thee a stranger, and took thee in? And the King shall answer and say unto them, Verily I say unto you, inasmuch as ye have done it unto one of the least of these my brethren, ye have done it unto me."

So He, Himself promises not only to sup with us, but He has told us that when we care for people in real need by sharing our eating and drinking with them, He considers that we have done this directly 'unto' Him. Jesus will communicate with you, as you eat alone, as you talk with Him and read His Word and think about Him, and will be with you in a real way. But there is a very important truth to recognize beyond this, and that is that the only way we can actually prepare a meal lovingly and with great attention to beauty and tastefulness, *for* Jesus, is to prepare it for "one of the least of these" His brethren. That added touch of beauty, the extra bit of work, the imaginative creative cooking, if done by the Christian with a conscious love for the Lord, is not only helpful to the individuals for whom we are cooking, but is accepted by the Lord as having been done for Him. How can it be anything but important, and utterly worthwhile?

However, Jesus limited this promise to hospitality "for one of the *least* of these". It is well to remember that when we do something for another person with love, and for the Lord, it is inevitably connected with doing it for someone who *would not normally be cared for in that way*. I really do not think that it means providing a big steak dinner for your husband's employer, or for some important client, or for someone you want to impress, or for someone who has entertained you and to whom you are returning the favour. I do not think when we are told to be "given to hospitality" it means that we are to be hospitable only to old friends. After all, we are told that if we are hospitable, in this special way, we *may* sometimes entertain "angels unawares". To do that we should have to be doing something special for a *stranger*. In any case, to do something directly for Him we would have to be doing it for "one of the least of these".

There was a railroad running through the town, Grove City, where Fran was pastor after he graduated from Seminary. Often hobos or tramps – rather derelict-looking older men, unshaven and ragged of clothing, who travelled by riding on the bottom of freight cars, or hidden inside an empty one – came to our back door, asking, "Cup of coffee, ma'am, and maybe some bread?"

"Wait a minute," I'd reply, "just sit down there, I'll fix you something." It was too dangerous to invite such a stranger in, alone with small children; but it would have been wrong to send him away.

I would get out a tray, put the kettle on, and look in the fridge for some left-over soup. Into a small pan would go the soup, with the gas on under it. I would cut bread, enough for two big sandwiches (not too thin, he'll be hungry) and wonder what sort of a home he had had when he was a little boy – and wonder who he is,

or whether maybe he is an angel in disguise! I would butter the bread, cut a lovely big tomato in even slices and pepper them, place them on the bread, and then decide to add bacon. I would sizzle one slice to fold over the tomato and add two leaves of lettuce. For a second sandwich I'd prepare him my own favourite: walnut halves stuck into the butter, salted on one slice, and then the second piece of buttered bread placed on top. A diagonal cut through the first sandwich showed red tomato and green lettuce attractively displayed in the slash. The walnuts crunched as the knife went diagonally through the second sandwich. Alternating these four triangles on a lovely dinner plate came next, with pickle trim on one, and parsley on the other. Now for the steaming hot soup left over from our lunch.* I would put a good bowl of this on the tray, and the children would help me fix a tiny bouquet of flowers nested in an ivy leaf.

"What'll he *think* of all that, Mummy?" Priscilla would ask with big, wondering eyes.

"Well, perhaps he'll remember something in his past – perhaps he had a very nice home once, where he had meals prepared for him. Anyway, he'll stop and *think*, and we'll give him this little Gospel of John to read while he is eating. He can take it away with him and, who knows, perhaps he'll do a *lot* of thinking, and some day, *believe*. Anyway, he may realize we care something about him as a person, and that's important."

Priscilla would hold the screen door open as I took it out, and watch his surprised face as he saw the tray.

"For *me*? Is this for me?"

"Yes, and the coffee will be ready in a minute, eat the soup first. This Gospel is for you, too. Take it with you. It really is very important."

All this for a tramp? Flower arrangements for a tramp on a rainy day? Why? Is it worth it? Is it just romantic? Does he even

---

* This was corn chowder, and here is the recipe:

Peel and cut up a dozen potatoes in tiny cubes, about $\frac{1}{4}$ in. square. Cut up half a dozen medium sized onions. Cook the onions and potatoes in water together, in a pan large enough for the finished soup – enough for about 8 people, or stretched for more! While these are cooking, cut up 6 or 8 pieces of fragrant smoked bacon in tiny pieces, and sizzle them in a pan until partially cooked and some of the fat is removed by melting into the pan. Add bacon to the potato onion broth, when the potatoes are soft. Then add a tin (or 'can', if you are American!) of corn, a packet of frozen corn, or four or five ears of fresh corn cooked and cut off the cob, and milk – about 3 to $3\frac{1}{2}$ pints. Now heat until almost boiling, with a quarter of a cup of cornflour (cornstarch) melted in cold water or milk added. Stir all the time to avoid burning the milk. Finally, add salt and black pepper or seasoned pepper and a lump of butter at the end. Serve with salty crackers. It is a wonderfully substantial soup with a sandwich or salad meal.

notice? If the Bible is true, this is the way to be doing something "unto Jesus", and at times perhaps to entertain an angel. Yes, there *are* other ways – there is the poor old woman who has no one to visit her in the hospital. There is the scrub woman, or 'char'. There is the juvenile delinquent. There are many people whom you may care for in a variety of ways. But as we are speaking about food, let us remember to prepare it beautifully for *each* person: in the family, to enhance communication and a feeling of loving care in the home; among friends and guests of all sorts; but also for strangers, who can do *nothing* in return for you, who seem truly to be "the least of these".

Often one is asked, "How does one get children to have compassion and love for others?" One important way is by demonstrating love and compassion in action, not just talking about it. I do not mean organizational action but human care, in taking time, thought, energy, imagination, and creativity to fulfil some total stranger's need. Nothing can be given in a 'course of study' which can substitute for the day to day observation on the part of the children in the home of a mother or father who truly treat human beings as human, and not machines. It is of course costly, in time and energy. "What a waste of time!" some might remark. But the 'waste' is what brings forth the most amazing results, many of which are hidden from us in this life, results in others living in and sharing the home; and results in unknown strangers, too.

My husband remarked one day, "Edith, our house is marked with a chalk mark. It's a sign tramps mark on foundations of houses letting other tramps know where they can get a hand-out." Yes, many came – one after another through the months. And the menu changed with each one, the flowers changed, the candle was lit at dusk or when the day was grey. Perhaps they 'took advantage' of us, perhaps the password was "There's an easy mark". But no matter. Several very positive things were taking place.

First of all, it was not hurting me. Indeed, it was developing me in various ways, and giving a kind of an outlet for creativity which was quite different, and real. Secondly, it was giving an opportunity to do something directly for the Lord, with love of Him uppermost. Thirdly, it was an opportunity to make direct contact with a few individuals out of a very large group, making up a small part of American life. Fourthly, it was part of our first child Priscilla's education which nothing else could give her.

The expression of 'Hidden Art' in the form of cooking and serving food, then, has a wide number of possibilities, and as everyone eats every day, it is no exaggeration to say that it affects every one of us. One could speculate as to what difference it would make if we all took this form of 'Hidden Art' seriously, with at least some degree of sensitivity for producing and enjoying the beauty which will increase and enhance communication.

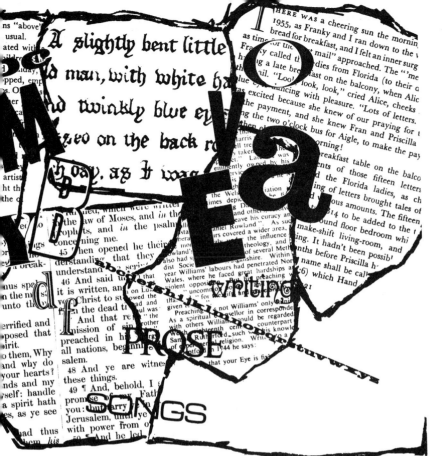

9. Writing – Prose and Poetry

Do you want to write, but find yourself plunged into washing dishes, nappies or windows? Have you felt you could express yourself in poetry if only you were not so busy selling houses? Have you had a manuscript on your mind, but never the time nor the quiet to get it on paper? Have you wanted to study journalism but had to go into law for one reason or another? Or have you had one rejection slip after another for books or articles, essays or poetry?

Is this the 'if only' of your life, which is making you into a bitter, dissatisfied and unfulfilled sort of person?

But factors such as these should not stop you from writing. If writing is your buried art form, disinter it and develop it. 'Hidden Art' in the area of writing can be developed in a practical way for the fulfilment of the writer and for the enjoyment and enrichment of the lives of family, friends, and casual contacts. Writing for enjoyment of expression – like music and painting – does not *need* an audience of more than one.

Writing is certainly a medium for communication, as all art forms are. It gives the opportunity for direct communication, for verbalizing thoughts and attitudes, for speaking truth and putting content into expression. Human communication in the form of words and language can be spoken or written. The written form can be read and re-read, thought about and read again. But one need not feel that writing has to be a career for it to be worth while, nor that it has to be prepared for by formal study before it can be fulfilling to the writer. If you feel you have an unrecognized talent for writing, or if you simply love to write and want to do it, my advice is *write*. But write without ambitious pride, which makes you feel it is a 'waste' to write what will never be published. Write to communicate with someone, even if it is literally only one person. It is not a *waste* to write beautiful prose or poetry for one person's eyes alone!

What can you write? Letters could well come first of all. We all have someone waiting for a letter, and each of us has someone thinking about him or her and wishing the mail would bring some sort of word, some message. The things you are burning to say, the words you want to use, and the ideas that flow as you are chopping wood, for instance, should not be bottled up only for publication. Write *now*. Communicate with someone *now*. Start by writing a letter to one person, and continue by writing to others who are waiting for a letter.

Perhaps there is only one person with whom you feel you could really communicate freely. Write to that one. Express yourself in prose or poetry. Then, sometimes it's good to write to someone with whom you have *not* as much freedom – and accept the challenge of making your ideas clear to that one. Write to someone who shares the same interests and has the same sensitivities, describing music, art and nature in ways you know will be appreciated. Or write to a person who has nothing in common with you, describing the view, giving the news of the day in vivid form. Write to an older friend, using your imagination as to what might interest that one and tie in with their past experience. Write to someone much younger, putting yourself in that person's place as you speak of a recent voyage across the sea – or across the street.

It is stimulating to write to a small child and give a description which would delight the little one, or tell a story as Beatrix Potter did in her first version of *Peter Rabbit*. Give the news of the past week or month to someone who is hungry for news of you. Describe what is going on in the form of a poem – not just what is going on inside your head and emotions but in the world around you.

Write to your parents if you are privileged still to have your parents. If they are thousands of miles away from you, try to bring them into the atmosphere and view of the country in which you live, so that when they finish reading your letter they will feel as if they had been spending the week with you. If they are thousands of philosophic miles separated from you, make an attempt to explain your understanding of the universe and your answer to the basic philosophic problems in life.

If you have no answers and are seeking, try to let them understand how serious your thinking is: even if they don't understand completely, at least try to formulate something in writing which will give them the feeling that they have been spending the evening with you, toasting their toes at some fireplace with a pot of steaming tea by their sides while you have talked earnestly to them, trying to explain your point of view, or the lack of it. Make a strong attempt to keep your parents 'with you' through letters as you travel and grow and change.

If you are a parent with children away from you for some reason or other – write, write, WRITE! 'Home' is made up of communication and growing relationships. If you haven't the

1953 95th Street.
Los Angeles 45.
California 90045.

2 ROTHER ROAD
LONDON
N.W.11.

Monday 5th

Dear Aunt Elizabeth,
This is to let you know
that Jabitha has had 7 kittens!

daily possibility of preparing artistic and delicious meals for your children, if you haven't your children there to awaken you in the night because they are sick, or need help of some sort; if your children are in boarding school because that is the custom of your society; if your kind of work transplants you into a foreign country, writing frequent and adequate letters is imperative, whether or not you have a talent for writing!

You talk to children when they are home, you mend their

clothes, serve refreshments to them and their friends, telephone the doctor, pick them up after school, help them with Latin or maths, take them to a football match – why, suddenly then, is a 'letter once a week' supposed to substitute for all that? It is not enough to pay·the bills and write casually once a week or twice a month. There are many shattered parents who have followed this pattern and seem 'bewildered' because they have lost all communication with their children.

It seems to me that writing letters to one's children should be thought of as taking the place of conversation at various times in the day. Many times it is not too much to write a daily letter, perhaps mailed twice or three times a week. Contact and communication with one's family should never be lost because of necessary separation.

If, on top of the absolutely essential need to keep in communication with the children, you also have a 'flair' for writing, then what better way is there to develop this than to let your imagination help you to work out a way to converse, tell stories, relate news and so on, to the child away from home. This must, of course, be done with sensitivity, so as to avoid things which will make the child more homesick. But it is possible to project yourself by imagination into the child's life, and talk of things which make him or her feel you are there in understanding with them. Amusing stories or tit-bits of news maintain the continuity of home life but do not make studying unbearable. When you send parcels, why not write about how you shopped for the contents? When vacation time draws near, one can begin to talk about preparation for the child's homecoming, and tell of some surprises in store. This will give the feeling that parents, too, are counting the days, just as the child is. And it is also possible to write of spiritual things, establishing a relationship which can continue in conversation when the homecoming takes place. It is a challenge to creative writing to write letters that capture interest, and which at the same time bring comfort and fulfil the need of communication for the child away from home. It also develops the writer, and fulfils a need there.

Naturally, writers of letters make mistakes, and each letter is not going to accomplish its purpose, any more than each meal is going to be the 'perfect meal' or each painting the 'perfect painting'. But each conversation is imperfect, too, and sometimes we end a conversation feeling that there has been no communication at all, and we might just as well have spent the evening sleeping.

So we need not wait to write the perfect letter. We need not delay communication because we feel there is a 'gap' which it is hard to cross. Instead, we can use our imagination and our ideas in personal communication with the child, rather than wait to share them with 'the public'.

I know young people who have had incredibly few letters from their parents during their years away at school and, unhappily, sometimes these parents were missionaries. Can we imagine what kind of attitude is likely to develop toward the beliefs of the parents if there is no attempt to communicate love, concern, ideas and beauty, in a way which comes across as a giving of *oneself*? All art, whether 'Hidden Art' or Career Art, involves *time*, a giving of time to produce the art, and the communication which results from the art, whatever form it takes. Human relationships cannot develop without communication. Understanding does not come in a vacuum of communication. Whether writing is one's 'Hidden Art' form or not, the communication of letters to one's children or parents or friends is entirely necessary to growing relationships. The person who is feeling frustrated because he cannot have a writing *career*, yet is not writing a profusion of letters, is really putting his personality in that restrictive 'cast' we have already talked about.

But supposing your whole family lives together, and your friends are all in the same locality – have you then no opportunity to write, short of having it as a career? Is there no way of developing your writing in the medium of real communication with people who are reading what you have written? Must your writing consist solely of a novel you 'hope' to work on during 'days off'? Or a collection of poems you keep under your mattress?

If you communicate in writing better than in speaking, if ideas for saying things in interesting ways come to you only with a typewriter under your fingers, or a pen in your hand, then *write*. You are making lunches for your children to carry to school, or your husband takes a lunch with him to work – why not make the

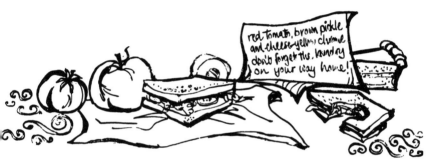

lunches communicate more than just the originality and deliciousness of the contents, by slipping in some surprise communication in writing? When the aluminium foil is unwrapped from the egg salad sandwich, why not let your husband find a witty note, or a clever poem, or a serious thought, or just a reminder that you are thinking of him? If rhymes and jingles come easily to your mind when you are washing dishes, write them down, and save them to stick into the little packets of nuts and raisins, or the celery and carrot sticks of the next day's lunch. You have a sense of humour that comes out with puns or little jokes that only the family would understand – why not write them and fold them up in the date bars that you have put in for dessert?

If communication in writing comes more easily to you than speaking does, then explain yourself in a note that you put under someone's plate at breakfast. If there has been a misunderstanding and you want to make "I'm sorry" into something a little more full and explicit, then write it in prose or poetry and pin it to the bathroom mirror, or clip it to the page of the favourite magazine that is being read. If you have an important letter it can go under the pillow to be read at bedtime when it is found just as the person is climbing in, before the light goes out.

I well remember the letters each of our three daughters wrote on the days of their weddings (the girls are four years apart in age, and of course their weddings were separated by some years, too). Priscilla wrote a letter that she put under Susan's pillow; then another for Debby and one for Franky. We thought it was so thoughtful of her as we saw what it meant to the younger children – Susan 16, Debby 12 and Franky 5. We finally went to bed, much later, still remarking how sensitive and thoughtful that had been on Pris's part, and how much difference it would make to the others, when we found ours, one to father, and one for me. There is something to be said at such a time which it is hard to put into a rushed spoken goodbye, which it is hard to express without sounding artificial, or seeming to break into a formal speech. A letter is the perfect medium, and can be kept and read over and over. Nothing else could possibly have given us what that letter did, right at that moment – not just months later, but right then. And when Susan was married, she too took time during the last days to prepare written messages to leave under the pillows of Debby and Franky, of Fran and myself. Debby had only three of us to write to, but her very satisfying letters were also under our pillows on the evening of her wedding day. There are only a few such important or crisis days in one's life, only a few such 'endings' to one section of life and beginnings to a new one, only a few such cataclysmic changes in the past pattern of family life and beginnings in a new sort of relationship. It is important for people to communicate their thoughts, feelings, gratitude and expectations in such a way as to build a bridge over the 'break' which is true and meaningful, rather than leave a misty gap of unsure hurts and undefined emotions.

Writing – Prose and Poetry

There are Christmas poems or letters to be written, and birthday messages in prose, poetry or jingle form. There are short plays that can be written for a family evening of entertainment, similar to the musical evenings of families with musical talents. There are biographical sketches and family history to write for amusement at family dinners, or for serious records to be kept through the years.

And then there is the diary to be kept. Some people like to jot down events day by day as a reminder, which would enable them to write something later. Others like to write a diary as a means of expression, not just news and historic facts as days go by, but thoughts, feelings and ideas, putting into words the daily struggles and an account of one's growing understanding of life, purpose and commitment. A diary can be a record of one's own growth culturally, spiritually, intellectually and physically. A diary can be an outlet for full expression philosophically and can help a person to understand himself, by being able to read back and see the gradual development in his own thinking.

For people living together in a school dormitory, apartment, or shared room, writing and then reading aloud what has been written and discussing it, can be not only an outlet and fulfilment for those who need to write and have the talent for writing, but it can be the basis for a much more complete discussion, because the reading of the written thoughts is apt to bring out into the arena of discussion more clearly the base upon which the writer has built his actions in life.

For anyone who wants to write, and hopes some day to publish what he or she has written, it is far more important to write than it is to study *about* writing. As you write for one person, or several, your desire to have that individual, who is known to you, understand your communication, helps you to express yourself in a manner which will also be understood by the 'unknown mass' called 'the public', which after all is only made up of a series of individuals.

143

For anyone who becomes confused in conversation, who gets rattled when eyes are upon him or when someone butts in, writing and outlining his ideas enables him to explain what he wants to say so much more easily, and enables the other people to know him, the real person who has disappeared behind the wall of incoherence. For that one, the gathering together of ideas in written form can be a communication to one individual, or a 'paper' to be read to the group.

For anyone whose mind wanders off to a dozen different thoughts in a dozen different directions when praying, it is often important to organize and present one's requests to God in writing. In such a case it is helpful to write one's praises, one's love for God, and one's thanksgiving. Such writing, in poetry, becomes hymns – but it is not necessary to start out to write hymns in order to come up with the most wonderfully true expressions of the reality of love and praise. Such reality comes in speaking directly to the God who is there, expecting Him to hear, to read and to receive the communication with understanding and appreciation. The greatest poetry is written to a person from a person; not written as beautiful sounding phrases of love or agony but written out of real love and real agony *to the person involved*. The greatest poetry or hymn of praise to God is surely written not with congregational singing in mind, but directly to Him as if no one else would ever hear. If no other person ever saw the prose or poetry written to God in real communication, which is real prayer, it would not matter. It is enough to have written it to Him. Writing for God's eyes alone, with the understanding of His existence, and the realization that He reads it, and the expectancy of His answer, is vertical communication in writing.

After all, God has communicated with us in writing. His Word, the Bible, is just this. It is what He would have us know, set down in written form. So writing our pleas, our praise, our prayers – this is *not* a one-sided communication. God has spoken. God is speaking. God will speak. God will hear, and He will answer. This is not artificial. It is real. It is not a psychological gimmick nor a therapeutic exercise, but a relaxed and protected comforting communication with one's Father, Shepherd, Friend, Counsellor and mighty God. He is Personal – and therefore we can speak and write to Him in a personal and intimate communication.

10. Drama

Perhaps you have always been good at acting, but you haven't had any opportunity to use or develop that talent, so you feel secretly that it is a completely hidden thing, which has been stuffed into a dark closet full of moth balls, waiting for the 'season' to come when it might have a usefulness again. Or perhaps you fancied yourself as an actor but no one else did, so (always unfairly) someone else got the leading part, and you had just to walk on and off the stage opening and shutting a door, or saying, "Yes, sir" and "No, sir" once or twice. Perhaps you feel you could be a great orator if only you were a statesman, or could have swayed crowds if only you had had the education and then the crowds in front of you to sway! You dream of yourself in some dramatic role, bringing tears to everyone's eyes, or you see yourself as a comedian causing people to double up with spontaneous laughter. *But –* here you are punching a clock in a factory day by day, cleaning the house, caring for children, working in a library, sterilizing instruments in a laboratory, planning a new building, driving a taxi, or doing research for a book on medieval history. So you feel cheated, frustrated, unappreciated, and undiscovered. And you try to pretend to yourself that you really are not affected by this hidden desire to use what you feel to be a talent, something you would really *enjoy* doing.

If you do nothing about this desire to use your dramatic ability, there is a frustration, and you put part of yourself in a 'plaster cast' which will stunt your personality rather than develop it. There is also the danger of your becoming a complaining, whining, warped sort of person with self-pity eating away inside you and coming out in caustic, jealous remarks. Or maybe you will lapse into day-dreams which take you out of real life into an unproductive fantasy.

In fact, it is wasteful not to use your talents to the full. It can be a form of pride not to use your abilities as 'Hidden Art' which will fulfil your own needs, and enrich the lives of others with whom you live, instead of submitting them to the frustrated you!

Reading aloud is the best outlet that I know of for hidden dramatic ability. It is the best development of speaking ability, and the least complicated exercise for the use of one's voice and expression.

I think reading aloud in a family, after dinner as you sit around the table and the candles burn down until they splutter out; around the fireplace as you read on and on and someone puts more twigs on the fire; in the rowing boat as you drift along slowly close to shore; in a country field under the only tree, looking over the endless cornfields and the blue sky; in an old fashioned porch in the twilight of a summer evening; in the cosiness of a home or cabin as the rain slashes against the windows; in an apartment in a city above the waves of human voices below; in the bedroom as the whole family is ready for bed and in pyjamas and robes, or already tucked in, listening sleepily together – is the most *together* thing a family can do. This is a far more uniting experience than being entertained by radio, TV or any sort of entertainment you *go* to, or sit and *watch*. You are plunged into the life of the characters in the book, you identify with another moment of history, another part of the world, another person's imagination – and you exchange glances of amusement, excitement, appreciation, understanding – or you laugh aloud together. You interject remarks, or stop to have an exchange of views or a conversation based on the characters or the events in the book. Whether it is with small children, adults, or a group of varied ages, there are questions or thoughts that simply burst out at times as the book is shared together, and which open up opportunities for knowing each other and each other's responses and attitudes in ways which no other 'entertainment' could ever do. Attitudes and ideas come out which might never be brought out in ordinary conversation. It gives the family a background for thinking and growing in their concepts and understanding, *together*, rather than always separately.

Reading together, with one person reading aloud, gives a depth of sharing which is a wonderful memory as years go on. A family relationship grows and is bound together with many kinds of 'thread'. Books can be bought through the months, be saved for vacation times together, be selected for nightly reading times, be planned for the stages of growth of small children and the growth in appreciation among adults. Even an expensive hard-back book is nothing compared to the cost of buying tickets for the family to go to some sort of entertainment. Books ought to be thought of as old friends in the family; therefore, whenever it is possible, children should be introduced to artistically prepared books. Again this is a step away from the 'plastic container throw-away' age which is overwhelming many today and causing people to cry out in alarm for the future.

Reading aloud gives the person reading a tremendous outlet and fulfilment for any dramatic ability he might have, with the possibility of identifying by voice and emotion with the characters in the story. There is the challenge of being prepared to change the voice as one's eye reads lines ahead of one's lips, and sees the speech of the next character. There is the skill of speaking with enough expression, yet not exaggerated; or reading without hesitation or emphasis on the wrong word; of not letting things drag, yet not skipping description, nor reading too quickly over an explanation that is necessary to the plot as it develops. There is the sudden decision to omit a word or two without letting the listeners notice a gap, and the choice of the lilt of voice needed to bring a poem or song alive.

Simply to complain or feel neglected or frustrated because one has no opportunity to be in a play, and yet never to read aloud to your room-mates, friends, family, the children next door, a sick child in the hospital, a blind person, or some elderly folk in a home, is really to prefer wallowing in self-pity, rather than having a very practical fulfilment for one's talent.

My father, who is now ninety-four, has always amused us with his ability as a mimic. He would pretend to be Paderewski, or an orchestra leader, or Charlie Chaplin. I can remember as a very small child saying, "Be funny, daddy, be *funny*" – anything in the line of mimicry would do! Throughout the years he has used this ability by reading aloud books with various accents in the speech of the characters. *Hyman Kaplan* – one of his favourite books, with its variety of accents of Brooklyn immigrants studying English for their exams toward naturalization papers – has been read aloud many, many times, and on my recent visit to him, a chapter of *Hyman Kaplan* was read to me again, as father stood

with one knee resting on a chair, and flipped over the pages of the
book. A bit later he pulled out *Winnie-the-Pooh* and read a portion
of it again, aloud to me. Father's long years have included twenty
as a missionary in China, about seven as a pastor in Newburgh,
about four in editorial work, and seventeen as a professor in Faith
Theological Seminary, and then seven as Treasurer and American
Representative for L'Abri. Yet his mimicry and dramatic ability
and his ability as a clown have not been squashed and in his
nineties they are still finding an outlet. There is still fulfilment
for him and pleasure for others.

For some groups of people, I would suggest reading aloud as

a good way of enjoying an evening together. Perhaps dinner together – and then reading. The book can be a history, biography or mystery story; it may be amusing, serious or educational. It would be possible to read a Shakespeare play, with each one taking a part, or to read a children's book for relaxation, and to gain a glimpse of the insights into life given in so many children's classics. It could be *Pilgrim's Progress*, or some other Christian book – and it could be the Bible read as the exciting Book it is, and not just as a duty. If there are adults living in the same house or who are frequently together, a book could be read over the period of a month or two as a regular 'together' thing. A book-reading evening could be accompanied by food appropriate to the season – fresh apples to munch as people lie comfortably on the rug, fresh strawberries to dip in a mound of powdered sugar as you sit in lawn chairs or sprawled on the grass – a provision for hunger and thirst, so that the exciting part will not be disturbed! It is a kind of embarking on a voyage, with food and drink on board: no need to interrupt the journey!

People ask, "What is your advice about bringing up children? What did you *do* as a family?" If there is any one thing I would stress as an answer it would be this: "I read aloud to the children, both individually and together." Reading together is one of the most important factors in a growing family relationship. Reading aloud is a kind of 'core' for the unity of a family.

We hear these expressions or read them as headlines in magazines and newspapers – The Age of Plastic, Family Life Disintegrating, Drug Threat Increasing, Pollution, Divorce on the Increase, Home Becoming an Obsolete Word. Is there anything that can be done about these titanic problems? What can I do about it? What can you do?

Of course the answer is a deeper thing than reading a book or putting a rose beside the bed or lighting a candle or throwing a log on the fire. Of course there has to be a real base for our own lives and for our ideas and morals. Of course we have to have a purpose for our life, and know that answers *do* exist, and that there really *is* someone 'at home' in the universe, a Person to give the answers, who has spoken and to whom we may go for advice and guidance. Of course there is no easy pushbutton answer, even for those who *do* have a base and do have assurance as to their relationship with the God who is there. Even deep and understanding Christians are still overwhelmed with the changing circumstances which surround them in bringing up a family today.

But this book is about 'Hidden Art', and the need of people who are in communication with the Creator to recognize their creative abilities and fulfil some of their talents in day-by-day life. And this *is* relevant to our depersonalized plastic age. I think it is valid to say that there must be some actual changes and some practical additions made to the day-by-day lives of many Christian families. This means starting when children are little, and not suddenly expecting to start with an almost adult teenager to give him in one year all he or she has missed during the past fourteen years. What I am talking about means taking our responsibilities and capabilities seriously. It means feeling that our ability to do things *should* be used in some way to make family life fun, and to enhance the relationships of people living together. To do this means working at it. A good marriage does not just fall out of a tree, by itself. A good family life and understanding, warm, rich, happy relationships within a family do not just spring up without someone working at it, someone who is not putting himself or herself first.

The plea for women to have 'time to be themselves' or 'time for fulfilling careers' is overworked. All that happens is that the psychiatrists get more patients than ever before. If people were less anxious to join a drama club or some other kind of 'fulfil yourself' activity and used their talents right in their homes, they would not only be more fulfilled when the children were two years old and they were capturing their attention with vivid and original ideas, but when the same children were eighteen years old they would not be wringing their hands so tragically at the complete lack of communication with them.

To chip away at marble and turn it into a marvellous piece of sculpture takes work, constant and patient. To 'sculpt' a life, in the midst of life itself, takes more work, is for longer periods of time, and needs far more patience. And reading is a 'tool' we ought not to ignore as well as a means to fulfilment at the same time.

I could not wait to begin reading to my first child, Priscilla. I am afraid I started before she could possibly understand what it was all about, but she enjoyed being talked to just the same. By the time she was eighteen months old she was clamouring every night for the same poem. It is *Over in the Meadow* by Olive A. Wadsworth and is a favourite with two-year-olds. My grand-daughter Natasha loves it and knows it by heart.

OVER IN THE MEADOW

Over in the meadow,
    In the sand, in the sun,
Lived an old mother–toad
    And her little toadie one.
"Wink," said the mother;
    "I wink," said the one;
So he winked and she blinked
    In the sand, in the sun.

Over in the meadow,
    Where the stream runs blue,
Lived an old mother–fish
    And her little fishes two;
"Swim," said the mother;

Drama

"We swim," said the two;
So they swam and they leaped
  Where the stream runs blue.

Over in the meadow,
  In a hole in a tree,
Lived an old mother-bluebird
  And her little birdies three.
"Sing," said the mother;
  "We sing," said the three;
So they sang and were glad,
  In the hole in the tree.

Over in the meadow,
  In the reeds on the shore,
Lived a mother-muskrat
  And her ratties four.
"Dive," said the mother;
  "We dive," said the four;
So they dived and they burrowed
  In the reeds on the shore.

Over in the meadow,
  In a snug bee-hive,
Lived a mother honey bee
  And her little bees five.
"Buzz," said the mother;
  "We buzz," said the five;
So they buzzed and they hummed
  In the snug bee-hive.

Over in the meadow,
  In a nest built of sticks,
Lived a black mother-crow

And her little crows six.
"Caw," said the mother;
  "We caw," said the six;
So they cawed and they called
  In their nest built of sticks.

Over in the meadow,
  Where the grass is so even,
Lived a gay mother-cricket
  And her little crickets seven.
"Chirp," said the mother;
  "We chirp," said the seven;
So they chirped cheery notes
  In the grass soft and even.

Over in the meadow,
  By the old mossy gate,
Lived a brown mother-lizard
  And her little lizards eight.
"Bask," said the mother;
  "We bask," said the eight;
So they basked in the sun
  On the old mossy gate.

Over in the meadow,
  Where the quiet pools shine,
Lived a green mother-frog
  And her little froggies nine.
"Croak," said the mother;
  "We croak," said the nine;
So they croaked and they splashed
  Where the quiet pools shine.

Drama

Over in the meadow,
    In a sly little den,
Lived a grey mother-spider
    And her little spiders ten.
"Spin," said the mother;
    "We spin," said the ten;
So they spun lace webs
    In their sly little den.

Olive A. Wadsworth

I always read this poem with a certain beat, and my foot still starts to tap as I say it that way in my head. I loved going all the way through to the last verse, with the ten spiders who lived with their mother.

So they spun lace webs
    In their sly little den.

Priscilla was four when Susan was born, and Susan got in on whatever I was reading to Priscilla. Pris wanted to hear everything I read to Susan, of course, even if she had heard it hundreds of times. When Debby came along four years later, she too was plunged into more advanced stories at a much earlier age, but she did not miss the beginners' ones, as we rocked and read nursery rhymes and pushed little cardboard Timmy back and forth for "Swim Timmy, Swim". Her understanding and taste developed by leaps and bounds, however, as she listened to her sister's stories, too.

I had a formula for reading, and also a very definite explanation of the difference in categories of books. My formula was to read something out of three classifications of books each evening, whenever possible. The first would be something from a variety of children's stories, classics, fairy stories, and so forth; then I would read something with a Christian message; and then finish with a Bible story – or, as they grew older, with the Bible itself.

157

It seemed to me this served as a real preparation for sleep, and a gentle cutting off from the activity of the day, as well as opening the way for questions and conversation about serious things. Prayers together at the end meant that the child prayed first, and then I prayed – and often the child would be asleep before I stopped praying. If not, I often sang a few hymns – the same ones each night.

I tried to explain the different kinds of books like this: "There are *four* kinds of books. First, fairy stories, which are make-believe and couldn't happen, but which are fun to think about and pretend are true. There are a lot of happy fairy stories, with animals that talk, or people only thumb high. Secondly, there are stories which *could* be true, which are just made up by the person writing; stories of little boys and girls, people doing things that people really *do* do, but not stories about people who really lived, just *stories*. Thirdly, there are stories about people who really *did* live and who did really *do* the things that are told about. These are called 'biographies', or true life stories. There are lots of people whose lives are interesting and different from ours, and who you'd enjoy hearing about.

"Fourthly, there is another book which is quite different from anything else. It is the Bible. The Bible is God speaking to man, God speaking to *us*, telling us true things that happened in the past, telling us things that happened before any man lived, telling us things about the future. But the Bible doesn't tell us only history and things that are going to happen, it also tells us how to know God, and how to become one of His children so that we can have eternal life. It tells us how to *live*, and helps us to know what to do. The Bible gives us comfort when we are sad, and strength when we are weak. Yes, the Bible is different from *any* other book in the whole world, and it is important to realize this – and also important to read it over and over again."

By the time we came to live in Switzerland, our reading was already a long-established thing, but because we had no 'next door neighbour' children to play with, no Sunday school with other children of the same age, no Girl Scout (Guide) or Brownie troops, we continually tried to make up for what they were missing by giving them much, much *more*! We read every evening around the fireplace in Chalet des Frênes, and then later around the granite living room stove in Chalet Bijou. By the time the girls were six, ten, and fourteen we had a 'mixed diet' of books which

we all enjoyed. There was always *Winnie-the-Pooh* to repeat in between other things, *Alice in Wonderland* and *The Wind in the Willows* and *The Water Babies*. There were the 'Anne' books of L. M. Montgomery, taking us to the atmosphere of Prince Edward Island in another moment of history. There was *The Pilgrim's Progress* on Sundays when we sat on the floor to eat our supper, picnic style, around the dining room opening of the granite stove in the living room.

When Franky was born Debby was seven. But it is amazing that the books that were read over the next few years were just as interesting to the entire family as to the youngest. We had discovered that the Beatrix Potter books never grow old, and Cicely M. Barker's *Flower Fairies* has not only lilting verses, but beautiful pictures and is a very good way of teaching the names and characteristics of basic flowers found in England. It is fun to watch a new person (of a year or two) being introduced to the Dick Bruna books, and nursery rhymes, but as time goes on

everyone is enjoying *The Borrowers Afloat*, and the other
'Borrowers' books; everyone likes to hear *Heidi* again, and to
follow the early American family life as it moves from one
pioneer area of the United States to another farther west in *Little
House in the Big Woods*, *House on the Prairie* and similar books by
Laura Ingalls Wilder. This author makes the whole family feel as
if they had just been churning butter, smoking meat, shooting
bears or braiding rugs. The simple pleasures and rigours of life in
the pioneer days are healthy antidotes for the twentieth-century
way of life! *Little Women* and *Little Men* are good to live through
too, as well as Kate Seredy's *The Chestery Oak* and *The Good
Master*. You can also take your children to early Cape Cod days in
Joseph Lincoln stories, or to the California coast among the
marvellous woods or on the beaches in Gene Stratton Porter
books with rich description of the deep woods, butterflies and
swamp life.

Romantic? Surely, it does not hurt to read the writing of
another period. And how are our children going to know anything about any other kind of standard or attitude than the one
by which they are surrounded, unless they read, or have read to
them something written long ago? To live through these books
together, to experience them as a family, is something quite vivid
and real, much much more real than reading alone. There is
something about *hearing* in someone's voice the conversations in
the books, sharing the emotions produced by the circumstances
which are being described, which gives one a greater involvement
or identification with all that is being read. Because of the greater
involvement, my theory is that the clamour and noise of the
present age are more thoroughly shut out. And there is no better
starting point for the father and mother to discuss Biblical
answers; many of Fran's deep discussions with our own children
had this very natural starting place.

As time goes on and the family gets older, one doesn't stop
reading. There are not only Paul Gallico's children's fairy stories,

but also his *Mrs Harris goes to Paris*, and the next two Mrs Harris books. There is the fun of sharing the experiences of *Three Men in a Boat*, and of going back and reading Charles Dickens aloud. There is *Stuart Little* and *Manx Mouse*, and then the Helen McGinnis spy stories which are also quite accurate historically. There are mystery stories to be mulled over together. After all, "I wonder who did do it?" is a shared kind of suspense. The value of our reading aloud together has been proved by the very high 'code of honesty' and fairness that has developed; an unwritten code. No one reads ahead in the story which we are all sharing, no matter how much their curiosity is whetted! And if "mother is reading that one with me", then another person, even a sister, does not *dare* to read it. It is not just a story to be read by who-ever comes along, it is a shared experience that must be waited for, until the person with whom it is being shared appears on the scene again. The series of books written by Opal Wheeler giving the lives of great music composers with emphasis on their child-hood, are accurate and have lovely black and white illustrations. They give a good base for arousing interest in the music these artists have composed.

What about the Christian books a child should get to know as he grows up? The Overseas Missionary Fellowship (formerly the China Inland Mission) has true stories for children, several very fine ones. The Dohnavur Fellowship has one for children, about their children in India. There are Patricia St John's stories, *Star of Light* and *Treasures in the Snow*, and the lovely *Sunshine Country* by Christina Roy (which is out of print, but one hopes some publisher will decide to reprint it). The imaginative stories of C. S. Lewis are important because he sees the reality of the supernatural and the supernatural battle. I am thinking here of his series of allegories for children, commencing with *The Lion, The Witch, and The Wardrobe*. Of course, these are imaginative and not 'real' but C. S. Lewis's idea of what the heavenly country may be like. Young people who are really well grounded in the teaching of the Bible will not get confused, and Lewis's approach really does something to make the supernatural seem not so far away and impossible. When C. S. Lewis wrote his Science Trilogy (three books) he similarly achieved that same breaking of the wall of impossibility for some adult people's thinking; the supernatural is right beside us. The ignoring or denying of the reality of the existence of God, and of angels; the attempt to live as if the universe were only a machine-like collection of atoms – this is destructive for any one human being and to human beings as a whole. Our children go into the world of school, newspapers, TV, magazines, conversations and modern books, and are deluged with an almost monolithic voice of unbelief and materialism. We ought not only to 'talk' – but try to take them and ourselves back into the hearing of *other* 'voices' as we shut out the 'world' and read.

But no reading is complete without some time spent together as a family in the reading of the Bible. 'Family Prayers' are extinct in so many Christian families today. There is always a meeting or a church activity to cause the family to fly off in ten directions, or parents to go out and leave baby-sitters. The need for a family life ought to be reconsidered and studied by each of us. Hard work and the sacrifice of time and energy are going to be needed if even a little step is going to be taken in the direction of rebuilding a true family 'oneness' again.

So an evening of reading should be concluded by some time spent reading the Bible and praying together, unless that was how it started. For young children, someone – mother or father – could well be reading for some length of time every bedtime, not just once in a while. And the few verses, the Bible story, the time of prayer, should be a part of that. However, the best setting for 'Family Prayers' is the meal-time, breakfast, lunch or supper, or even all three! This is when there should be a meaningful reading of some Bible verses, a time for a question or two, and real prayer for the real needs of the family; not superficial prayer, but the real spiritual, the immediate material and the individual psychological needs brought out and the need recognized for direction and guidance by God in the choices affecting the family.

Are 'Family Prayers' a long way off from the 'Hidden Art' of drama, and talent in expression and speech? Not a bit of it. Imagine reading, with expression, the story of Daniel in the lion's den, or the three men in the furnace, or of Jonah, or Elijah calling down fire on his altar, or Peter being prayed for as he was in prison, or of Paul and Silas. I wish you could watch my daughters Priscilla, Susan or Debby teach the Bible, or read it to their children, or to the ones they teach at Sunday school here in Switzerland or in England. It is a medium for all the dramatic ability they have and they transfer this enthusiasm and excitement to the wide-eyed children they are teaching! This enthusiasm is not artificial or worked-up but real because of the reality of the assurance that the Bible is true and important. If you really believe that the Bible is true and you begin to teach it and relate its stories to an audience of children or adults, no matter how 'humble' the gathering, you will have no need to worry about fulfilment for your talents of story-telling or portrayal of emotion. The real emotion will come and the talent will be employed in making it real to others. And, incidentally, your own need in this area will begin to be fulfilled.

11. Creative Recreation

Creative recreation, in my personal definition, can be thought of in two ways. Firstly, it is recreation which produces creative results, stimulates creativity, refreshes one's ideas and stirs one to 'produce'. Secondly, it is recreation which is the *result* of original ideas, creative because someone has creatively *planned* an evening, a day, an occupation which in itself is fresh and different.

People differ so tremendously in what recreation does for them that one could not give hard and fast rules as to what would stimulate creativity. However, it does seem to me that to get away from the miles of concrete in cities, to leave the hum of voices and

screech of machines; to get out of reach of the advertising in its various forms so cleverly designed to crash into one's thinking with subtle or open suggestions to think or plan differently; to get out of the earshot of music; to get away from the disturbances and influence of men, planned or unplanned, and to find a place where one is open to influence only from the sky, the wind, the clouds coming up from the valley or closing in from the mountain peaks, the sparkle of snow in the sun, the marvel of light filtering through trees, or the sound of a waterfall splashing on rocks, or birds singing before sunrise, or the crickets' special song at twilight – this is to give one the possibility for some original thinking, for getting a few fresh ideas, for feeling inspired to some form of creativity.

People are not only spoiling nature and the earth, but they are also insulating themselves from it. They always have a building, a street, a car, a terrace paved with tile, or *something* between themselves and the earth. Man was made to relate to the things in the earth, mineral as well as plant, oxygen as well as animals. However, although everything we find in 'civilization' has come from, or has been produced out of the raw materials existing in the earth, still it seems we have become more and more separated from the basic things of the earth.

For instance, synthetic materials and fabrics, even though they do come from combinations of atoms in certain patterns and 'natural fabrics' from other combinations (if you want to think of it that way), do *not* give us the same direct feeling of interacting with, or relating to, 'nature'. One feels the softness of lamb's wool and thinks of sheep grazing on Scottish hills among the heather and gorse. One irons linen until it is crisp and ready to hang up and tries to remember what one has heard of growing flax. Wherever one lives in the world, one has some idea of cotton bursting its shell in a froth of white, whether one is being impressed by the bolt of imported Egyptian cotton one is looking at in selecting material for a summer dress, or being told that the sheets are pure cotton. There is some sort of a contact with the raw materials of the *earth*, which synthetic and rather mysterious combinations do not give.

During my early childhood in China I was given silk worms, and was taught to cut up the tenderest of mulberry leaves in tiny bits with scissors. The worms crawled all over the bits of leaves, eating their way right through them. As they grew I was told they could eat larger leaves and larger pieces. Finally they were given whole leaves, as they became mature. Then one day the first cocoon was in the process of being spun by the first worm. Others followed, until finally silk worms had affixed themselves to the branches that had been put in for that purpose, and my daily job of cleaning the basket and preparing leaves was at an end. My Chinese *amah* (nurse) next showed me how to test the cocoons, stretching them between thumb and forefinger and gazing at the transparency against a light, teaching me just what to look for in making the judgement 'ready' or 'not ready'.

As I remember it, a professional woman came to our compound with her equipment to spin off the silk on to her spinning wheel. The spun silk, on spools, was then taken to be woven and finally I had a dress made of the material: a Chinese silk with a kind of damask pattern. Not only was I proud of the beauty of the dress because I liked the blue and softness of the silk, but it was totally satisfying and complete. It had come from the worms, and all those leaves, and I had had a part in much of it and had followed the whole process. Silk relates for me to that experience of 'earthiness' and interaction with the basic processes, and I can never feel the same about a synthetic material. Somehow synthetics seem a step away from the basic simplicity of the production of wool, cotton, linen and silk: a step away in somewhat the same way as a highway, a car or a building separates man from experiencing the 'earth'. Man does not have the same healthy refreshment for his nervous or his physical system if he never gets his feet on the earth, and his eyes, nostrils, ears, and taste buds free from the sights, sounds, flavours and smells of machine, concrete, exhaust and other non-natural things.

What am I driving at? I believe it would make a great difference to city dwellers, and even small-town dwellers, who are always in automobiles or houses, factories or stores, theatres or churches, aeroplanes, buses, or trains, who never walk, run, or swim anywhere, or ride horseback or canoe down a river – if they *would*, for a change! What a transformation there would be if they were to walk, ride or swim to get somewhere, instead of going behind a motor with their bodies insulated from land or sea!

If you have not done it recently, try getting out somewhere into the fields or woods, even country lanes, or on hard-packed sand running along a shore. Walk under trees after snow, or while it is still snowing, and listen to the quiet; quiet so still that you can hear the gentle plop of a bit of snow falling from one branch to another. Discover a bit of moss still green as it sheds its snow and seems to hint of spring to come, clinging to the base of a tree. Walk for an hour, two hours, along tiny paths, up steep hills, following a stream bed. Get out beyond the town, and stand watching the sunset, getting the feel, for a moment at least, of what it might have been like to be there as an early settler, battling the elements instead of the smog!

It takes will power and determination in today's world to take a day off to walk or hike, to become tired yet refreshed through physical effort in the setting of the beauty and quietness of nature. Physical tiredness and mental and nervous tiredness are not the same thing. Exercise such as walking where the atmosphere is totally different from one's daily surroundings, and where the beauty of nature captures one's interest and thoughts, can do more to *rest* one than sleeping on a couch or bed.

This kind of 'rest', a sliding away of the tensions and worries, a change of perspective, an emptying of the mind of the daily schedule, releases creative energy, creative thoughts and ideas. Walk alone, walk with one other person, walk with several others, walk with your family. It is amazing how far you can get in one day. Miles can be covered across fields, beside lakes, along marshy lands, over gently rolling farm land, through orchards and vine-yards, up and over hills. One seems to walk through history as one scrambles over Welsh rocks and stubbly grass where sheep graze and old churches and their graveyards tell of the people who walked here years ago. Wonderfully historic houses and churches can be visited by foot in the English countryside, with so much contact with the quiet of the country itself as one walks through secluded spots to stop and picnic and perhaps sleep, in a warm summer sun. Thoughts begin to come, as one sits to rest and watches a butterfly followed by a cricket and several other fas-cinating insects alight on one's foot or leg. Thoughts are followed by ideas: creative ideas, as one notices the tiny details of plant, flower and insect, and listens to the soft noises all around, broken by the louder call of birds.

It is in nature, among the things which God has created, desig-ned and brought forth Himself, that we are in the most natural atmosphere to be inspired. Creative ideas are apt to flow in the midst of the creativity expressed in God's creation, as one is

temporarily separated from the confusion of conflicting voices which would separate us from the simple basic realities of what 'is' – and this is especially true today, when so much of what man builds, paints and writes, not only has no place for God but has no place for nature or man either.

New ideas for writing books; words and music for a song; poetry that flows forth; colour schemes for decorating a room; colour combinations for the children's new dresses; subject matter for a sketch; blends of colour in painting a canvas; designs for your next suit; a plan for landscaping your own piece of ground; a method for planting which would catch the sun for longer periods of the day; new combinations of vegetables for dinner; an idea for capturing some of the wood's or the stream's atmosphere on your table as you see things you can gather with your hands, and 'see' in your imagination the things you are going to do with them; thoughts of deep philosophical variety; thoughts of how to get ideas across in a play or through photography; fresh ways of communicating with your children; a brainwave as to how to get the family all together – all this, and more, can be stirred up, flash into your head, grow slowly, begin to take form in your mind as you walk.

It is good to have special clothing for your walking, a special time selected for regular walking and some idea of where you can most quickly be away from the town and out into nature. Wherever you live, it is usually possible to get out where you can be on the earth, among rocks and trees, fields and bushes, desert or seashore.

Fran and I have old ski jackets, knee breeches with woollen knee socks and boots that lace up tightly and are big enough for an extra pair of socks. The boots have good, thick, mountain climbing soles. We do not need to be climbing to appreciate these soles. I have found that the boots make one feel quite protected from sharp stones and sudden slippery places, but also give one the sense of having seven league boots – that is, that the boots are carrying one along in the way the everyday shoes just cannot do. Even when I am very tired and feel I cannot make it, there is something about getting into all the walking togs, which in itself makes me feel ready to be refreshed by walking! The zipper pockets of the jackets can be filled with a variety of things which give the feeling of setting forth into the 'wilds' of nature, prepared for any emergency. This gives an air of adventure akin to being hundreds of miles away – quite different from walking to the grocery store or post office on any other day. A few squares of sesame seed and honey are what we like (you may prefer chocolate), a plastic bag of almonds and raisins, another of dried apricots – a supply of food enough to stave off hunger until a tea room can be found, or a store where bread and cheese can be picked up for a lunch in the first village one comes across. Some plasters, some antiseptic for scratches or bites, a railroad timetable, a handkerchief for many uses, a thin plastic raincoat to be unfolded in case of storm, a comb, and a small book are among the things with which we stuff our pockets.

There is great freedom about walking wherever your feet take you, not rushing past the scenery, not being bound to the roads, a feeling of conquering the countryside when you look back to see how far you have come, and yet a privacy and protection from the intrusion of other people. You can have the feeling of having covered many miles, and having been far away from everything for a long time, in just one day. However, the adventure is heightened if one stops in a village or in overnight accommodation, having come on foot, with no transportation. There is something about that combination of being in the woods or fields, with only one's feet for transportation, and then sleeping away from home, which cannot be found in other forms of travel. If one

carried a sleeping bag and slept outdoors it would be even more so perhaps – but only if there could be that 'primitive' travel by foot, ski, snowshoe, horseback, canoe, or maybe, as a close 'runner up', the bicycle (*not* with a motor) if time is taken to get off and into the woods during the ride. Anything but 'foot' limits one to certain paths, roads, or streams. If you do not trust your memory, a scrap of paper and a bit of pencil will keep you from forgetting your bursts of ideas, as you jot down enough to remind you when you get back.

All of this relates to the first half of my definition: recreation which produces creative results, which stimulates creativity, which refreshes one's ideas and stirs one up to produce. Now for the second way of thinking of creative recreation.

Whatever your creative talents are and however limited you feel you have been in using them, the necessary release of these talents can be employed in planning recreation for others. If you are bored or feel a dullness and lethargy creeping over you or you feel a bit depressed; or if you feel very excited and happy for no special reason at all, but it makes you want to do something special; if you realize that everyone is getting into a rut of doing the same thing every day and accepting packaged, ready-made, plastic recreation – then create something new and different. Whatever the circumstances, the very planning, preparing, anticipating and executing will fulfil something in *you*, as well as provide something to refresh and bring fun to the others for whom you provide a surprise, or an original time of recreation, born out of your creativity.

When our children were small we had what I called 'Treasure Hunt Meals'. Far from being a birthday or a special occasion when the announcement was made, it was usually quite the opposite, a time when I felt there was some friction, or a disappointment or sadness about something. "Supper tonight will be a Treasure Hunt", I'd announce, and the rest of the afternoon was a time of anticipation on the part of the children. I would sit down with a pad of paper, and think – begin writing notes, then go around the house looking, and then come back and write some more. It would take a lot of planning – but it was fun trying to think of new and different ways of wording the clues and new and different places to hide them, and new and different places and ways to serve the meal. There would be about ten clues before the first 'treasure' was found, and then another ten for the next course, and as many as I had time to make for the next!

Each clue, of course, tells where the next clue is to be found. The wording can be as different as your imagination will allow: in rhyme, in riddles to guess, or just simply describing the place to look. Of course, the kind of clues one leaves partly depends on the age of the children. If the children differ greatly in age, there should be 'picture clues' for the younger ones and each clue should be put in an envelope for the child, with his or her name on it. If they are about the same age one clue will do in each place. The simplicity or the elaborateness of the whole game can differ from time to time, depending on how clever you feel at the moment. It is a challenge to arrange a series with variety and unexpected endings – or with the clever blending together of jingles; or not so clever, as children are not critical, and you can constantly try new things.

"Under a green chair, near the stair, just look hard, you'll find the card."

"Pull up a small rug, you'll find a bug." (That note will be cut in the shape of a ladybug – ladybird in England – or have pictures of some on it.)

"Now you'll have to think. What's under the kitchen sink? Open the box. Read what's written in *ink*." (The next clue can have something written in ink, and something written in pencil and they must read only the part in ink to get to the right place.)

"Now look in Susan's bed. It's where she puts her head. The right part will be in red." (The next clue will have the right information in red, and some foolish little thing written in green.)

"A tisket a tasket, a green and yellow basket . . . where do you think you'll find it?"

"Look hard behind the sofa (divan) now, and then sit down to eat it, eat it, eat it" (to be sung as in the game).

The first course might be grapefruit, oranges and banana cut up and put back into half grapefruit shells (scooped out to form a dish), all sitting in a decorated basket (green and yellow) with spoons and napkins carefully in them, too. Plates would be in the side of the basket (decorative paper plates) and we would sit on the floor to eat, in a circle.

Then the next clue would be given, and they would be off

looking again while I went to the oven to make sure all was in readiness for the main course. Clues would lead them to the top floor and meantime I would quickly set the kitchen table where the main course was to be eaten. Clues would lead them to the oven where individual chicken pies would be bubbling and a wooden bowl of chef's salad (lettuce, tomato wedges, and any other available greens chopped with parsley, chives and cucumber slices added, tossed with their favourite dressing) would be found behind a cupboard door, with another clue.

The next clues would lead them to their pyjamas, all folded in a box in some unexpected place like a window-seat in the dining room. They would take the hint, put them on, and race to put their clothes away (this would be ordered in the clue) before they looked for the next clue. The final clue would lead them to the living room fire-place, where a box had appeared at the appropriate moment, to be opened, and inside would be cones, with a note saying that if they sang a certain song, ice cream would appear! Of course, as they sang I went to the fridge for the cream. While they were eating the ice cream cones, I would read a story, and then they would have family prayers, clean their teeth and off to bed!

There were endless varieties of meal hunts! Hunts that would take them from bush to bush outdoors in the summer time, after supper, and the 'surprise' would be a water melon; hunts that would take them to a box of bubble bath, on a hot sticky summer day; hunts that would take them to a new book, the story for that night; hunts that would take them to the bedroom where a picnic in a shoe box, decorated for each one, would give them individually served suppers that night.

Your own creative abilities and ideas would give variety to this idea. Jigsaw puzzles can be made of a picture with the message printed on it and when the puzzle is all finished, the secret will be told. Creative recreation needs a changed mentality to get started: one which does not just shove the children in front of a TV set to keep them quiet but thinks of the challenge as something which will develop into a *person* and at the same time give memories of a childhood to the children which is their *own* childhood, not just a looking into the lives of others on a screen. With variations, the same sort of thing can be done for people of any age.

Time? Yes, it takes time. But not as much as you might think. Plans are laid while one washes dishes, preparations are made when one is waiting for the cake to finish baking. Notes, ideas, plans, can be jotted down and kept ready for the opportune moment. And it is time well spent in really having a *family* life, in making home more fun than any other place, which makes other 'attractions' seem boring by contrast.

If there is an art museum in your town or anywhere nearby, a family tour of the museum could be a regular occasion, not a once-in-a-life-time occurrence. These trips should differ. At times it is a matter of walking through and commenting. At other times it is a matter of sitting in front of a fountain or a favourite spot just to look, to keep quiet and think. This is not only relaxing for the whole family, but gives them time to look at details of beauty not just as a 'sight' to be observed with superficiality but as things to be absorbed and enjoyed. The art museum becomes a part of the memory of childhood and gives the same advantages as having a Rembrandt in the house! Art books at home can be looked at and discussed and then 'discoveries' can be made when familiar names are found in the museum. Games can be made of this. Children can also sit with a sketch pad and sketch in the museum and have a little 'exhibition' of their own when they get back home.

Creative recreation as the result of original ideas need not depend simply on one person in a family or a group. If one person begins really to develop in these areas and produces things which others join in there will soon be someone else coming up with an idea.

Susan used to love to make puppet shows or have plays in which the other two, Priscilla and Debby, either had their parts too, or became the audience. Susan's puppets were home-made creations of her own, which involved making the faces, sewing clothing for them, and making a stage and curtains and so on. When we got our first tape-recorder, Priscilla became a radio announcer and made all sorts of programmes, which Susan and Debby were able to take part in. Then they would sit and listen to

their own programmes, and invite us, too. They included news announcements, music, story hours, plays, advice to the lovelorn, recipes – and sermons! There was no end to the ideas involved on the part of the three girls as they thought up new things, prepared them and invited us to be their audience.

Later, when Franky was about the same age, he spent hours putting radio programmes together on tape, and as the girls were then grown up, Fran would listen to as many of them as he could squeeze into his busy schedule. Both with the girls and Franky, we always tried to find time to share in their creative productions. Children, like artists and musicians, need an audience to encourage their creativity to grow. Christians can consciously provide such an audience for all ages and all levels of talent, knowing that creativity springs from being made in the image of God.

How can children possibly have a creative childhood if they sit in front of television for hours every week without exercise of body or development of ingenuity and their own creativity? In our family we have now come to another generation, and it is satisfying to see Susan teaching her daughters to make dolls out of empty plastic bottles, with cloth heads, eyes and mouths painted on and clothing made by the children, and in Priscilla's family, Elizabee and Becky (six and eight years old) are writing a book in French and English.

One needs to fight to prevent creativity being killed. Children are naturally creative, but it needs encouragement. They need to become aware that they were made in the image of the Creator, and are meant to be creative. They can begin to understand that there is a difference between the infinite (like God) and the finite (like man), so that they appreciate that they cannot do *everything*, but they need not just give up and 'sit', living other people's lives on the screen and 'graduating' one day to the place where they have no interest, no enthusiasm and no excitement, like so many of today's 'drop outs' who have dropped out of creativity as well as formal education. Unhappily, many teachers, as well as parents – who are the first teachers – have 'dropped out' too; out of the real universe, which is one in which personality has meaning because man was made in the image of a Personal God. The impersonal universe of man's making is one which does not produce a base for creativity.

But Christians, who do have a base for creativity, as well as other marks of personality, are very often *not* the most creative people nor the ones who produce an atmosphere for creativity.

Yet they have a solemn responsibility in this: to themselves, to others and to the God who created them.

Some sort of relaxation is needed by everyone, that seems clear. Certainly, then, *part* of that relaxation should equip and prepare us to be more creative in our work and lives; and part of it ought to be the result of creative ideas which are growing and multiplying all the time.

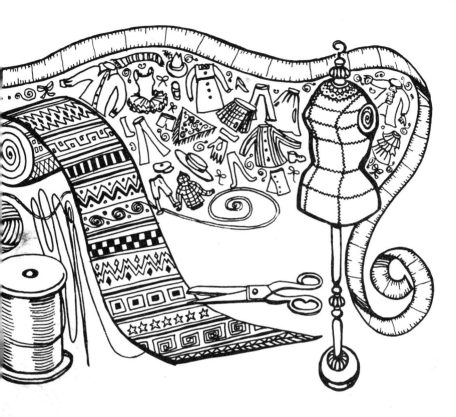

12. Clothing

Since ancient times, people have been concerned to dress 'correctly', which usually just means dressing in the fashion of the period. Attached to this whole subject of fashion, however, are many other topics. Does it matter how we dress? Is it a sign of spirituality to be dowdy? Are certain clothes and styles positively 'wrong'? And are others positively 'right'? Certainly some Christians have asked these questions, and sometimes they have come up with some very strange answers.

There are those who have contended that certain colours are

'worldly', that certain lengths of dress are not 'Christian'; others say that wearing buttons brings pride, and so they never fasten their clothing with buttons. There are those who say that trousers for women are not 'Christian', though in some parts of the world all women wear trousers and the men wear the loose tunics. There are groups who teach that flowered materials are not 'spiritual' but that plain brown, grey and black are, and others have insisted that everyone should wear the same style, children and parents, from generation to generation, feeling that *change* is wrong. Some think that Christians should not look fashionable, and that there is virtue in appearing dowdy. Others have as a standard a certain period of time – never the present time, but some point in the past – as the right way to dress for a Christian, so they always look 'out of date', although they never consider that if the clock suddenly turned back, they would be the ones who were the most 'stylish' and all others would be strange and not 'with it'.

Going back a bit to the beginning of clothing, one finds that God clothed Adam and Eve after the Fall, with leather, fur and perhaps suede. Anyway, it was with the skins of animals that Adam and Eve were clothed when they left the gorgeous garden, and began to live in a now 'spoiled' universe. Perhaps they had leopard skin tunics. Who knows how beautiful the skins were!

Much later, God spoke through His Son to tell Christians that His children are not to worry about their supplies of food, drink and clothing. It is an admonition to put the will of God first and not the gain of material things.

However, in considering this strong admonition to put God first and to seek His righteousness, we should notice carefully what Christ actually said. "Think of the flowers, the lilies of the field, which do not do any work to gain anything, yet they are more beautifully clothed than King Solomon when he was at his height of glory. Therefore, if God can so beautifully clothe the flowers of the field, which only last a short time and then are cut down, how much more shall He clothe you, oh you of little faith?"

Clothing

Usually when preachers deal with this portion of the Bible, they stress the aspect of trusting God to provide what is needed, and being willing to do His will and follow His leading, no matter how foolish it may seem financially in the eyes of men. Indeed, this is a passage which has always helped me personally to live on the basis of prayer. It encourages the Christian to pray for his daily needs, and follow the Lord's plan for the use of his life, without what men might call 'security'. The security of having God as one's Father is supposed to be taken literally as the best security of all.

However, as we are thinking of clothing in the context of creativity, this passage also clearly says something else. It tells us to consider or think about (look at with our eyes and make some conclusions with our brains) the *fields full of flowers*. That is the starting place – look at and consider the fields! The fields I know best are the fields of Switzerland – a riot of colours – a fantastic variety of shape and textures. Christ tells me to look at the fields above Montreux, white as snow with the bursting forth of the narcissus, and lean down to examine one closely. The fragrance will cause you to breathe deeply, breathe again and sigh. What perfume! Then there is the velvet of creamy white petals, deepening into yellow in the centre and the pale and then darker green of the stem and leaves. One can think only of a wedding dress with the shining blonde hair of a young bride falling against the satin. I am to look at a field of daffodils swaying in the early morning breeze above Champéry, bright yellow of cup, paler yellow of petals and the perfect green to set them off the thick growth of leaves. One sees a young bridesmaid or two, following the bride, with yellow silk taffeta dresses standing crisply out around their feet, walking down a green carpeted aisle. Or up in the high mountains on a hike, in July or August, I find the single gentians – and then suddenly patches of ground absolutely carpeted with gentians, deep purple, sitting on the ground with small leaves holding them as if in green hands. Could Solomon in purple velvet be as beautifully clothed as these high mountain stemless flowers sitting on the dry stony ground? Then I am to walk through paths (not crushing the beauty of the fields) and look out over the slopes around Huémoz in June, before the farmers cut the hay. Hay? Is this just the food of cows? Who can count the variety of flowers? Daisies with their white petals vying with each other for size and perfection; bluebells of delicate texture and colour lined up on a stem like tiny girls in blue uniforms of some fairy school; dandelions in shaggy brilliance; pale pink wild snapdragons, Queen Anne's lace so tall and huge one thinks it must be a giant's variety; violets of every shade, tiny pansies, and many many more. Crocuses repeat themselves with a second crop in these fields when the grass and flowers are still low, in spring before the growth comes, and then again after the second cutting in the autumn. Never is there a time with no colour, texture, shape, fragrance or beauty to 'consider'.

"Wherefore, if God so clothe the grass of the field" – *God* clothed the grass like this. God the Creator made the beauty of colour, texture and variety of form of the flowers. We were told so elsewhere, but now we are told here that He not only created the flowers but that we can think of this in relationship to our clothing. God the Creator, Designer and Artist was also the first dress designer! Yes, we can *see* the kind of clothing God designs when we look at the flowers. Think of roses, begonias, tulips, hyacinths, water lilies, lilies of the valley and Easter lilies. Think of orchids, poppies, chrysanthemums, wisteria, arbutus or clover. Think of ageratum, pansies, petunias, geraniums, iris, phlox, morning glories, gardenias and carnations. Is there any pattern that is the only 'right' pattern for a flower? Is there any colour that is the only 'right' colour for a flower? Is there any greater variety of colour, form or texture than in the realm of the flowers of the world? God designed the flowers and caused them to continue through the centuries so that we can have before us examples of His patterns for our clothing! Flowers are the miniature patterns left for us to examine from year to year, from century to century.

Clothing

The point may seem strained, but in fact it is what Christ said:
"Consider the lilies (the flowers) of the field . . . Wherefore if
God so clothe the grass of the field . . . even Solomon in all his
glory was not arrayed (not *dressed*) like one of these." The con-
nection is made even more strikingly clear in the next sentence:
"Wherefore, if God so clothe the grass of the field which today is
and tomorrow is cast out, shall he not so much more *clothe* you, O
ye of little faith?" He is emphasizing that we are to trust Him to
provide us with the necessary clothing to cover us and keep us
warm, it is true: but He is claiming much more than simple
'utility', since He says that He who designed the clothing seen on
the flowers is the same One who will provide for us.

We must not forget the form in which Jesus put the promise –
"*How much more*" will He clothe us. He loves us and considers us
more important than the grass and flowers. We are personalities
who will live eternally. We are personal and so have the marks of
personality, including a capability for appreciating beauty and
creating it. We are to be perfectly fulfilled one day in the future.
But now God, who indicates in other parts of the Bible that we are
to be fed, have shelter, have human companionship and fulfilment
of our physical needs, tells us not to worry about our clothing
because if we put Him and His kingdom first He will see that we
have the things we need. And I feel He certainly does not mean
that those things are to be ugly: ugly clothing, ugly houses, or ugly
and unpalatable food! "For your heavenly Father knoweth that ye
have need of all these things. But seek ye first the kingdom of God,
and his righteousness; and all these things shall be added unto
you."

He who created us, who created the universe, who created the
fruits and vegetables, who created the flowers and 'clothed' them
in beauty, is the One who is telling us that we need not worry
about food, drink or clothing. He will take care of them. He gives
us food, shelter and clothing spiritually, now and always. He
gives us food, shelter and 'clothing' in the area of relationships we

have with other human beings. He gives us the literal food, also, the literal shelter, and the clothing for this present time.

So surely the question of a Christian living aesthetically, artistically and creatively comes into the area of clothing, too, does it not? Is it not important that a Christian represent in his clothing, the One in whose image he is made? Spiritually, we are clothed in the white linen robes which are the righteousness of Christ, and that is more important than fashion. But is there any reason why a child of the One who designed, created, brought forth and *clothed* the flowers should set out to look ugly and drab? Are we representing Him by being unattractive?

What about modesty, then? What about being willing to go without? What about sharing, being unselfish and putting other people first? None of these things needs to be neglected, as one thinks of clothing as a creative part of life. Modesty needs to be considered. We must be willing to go without material things, among them the money to buy *all* that we want in clothing. We do need to share in this area, and give to other people too. None of this is negated by realizing that beauty is important, that beauty, artistry and creativeness can come into the area of clothing. Whether we are providing clothing for ourselves, our children, a friend, or the 'stranger' in our home, the aspect of beauty, of 'considering the flowers', should enter in. We who are dressing ourselves and our children, providing for missionaries or friends, making things for orphans or refugees should 'consider the flowers', the lilies of the field, and consider it our part, as finite imperfect human beings, to be as creative as we have the talent to be!

What about styles? They change. Obviously geographical areas of the earth differ. One could not wear the same clothing in the ice and snow of Alaska as in the heat of India. One could not wear the same clothing in the dry desert as in the rainy season of the tropics. To say there is a general 'right' or 'wrong' in the kind of clothing worn, is to ignore the fact that one must wear some kind of a bathing costume in order to swim ten miles, and one must wear ski trousers to ski ten miles in the depth of winter. One must wear a certain kind of deep swimmer's rubber suit to go down to the depths possible in skin diving and one must wear a certain kind of attire to climb the Matterhorn.

Bare feet walking on wet sand, bare feet running on close cropped grass, bare feet shuffling through dry leaves, bare feet stepping on soft spongy moss, bare feet skipping on cool tiles – what is wrong with bare feet? Nothing, in the right setting. Sandals protecting feet from hot sand, sandals protecting feet from sharp glass, sandals protecting feet from hookworm eggs – what is wrong with sandals? Or thick boots fastened on skis, tramping through a marsh, on a river fishing expedition? Or smart shoes giving pleasure to a tired domestic worker; or satisfaction to a child who has waited to be big enough for a particular kind; or joy to a working girl as she spends her first pay; or confidence to a man applying for his first job? What is wrong with smart shoes? Nothing – in the right setting.

But is it wrong to be 'in fashion', to watch fashion changes and change one's pattern of clothing? Or is it better to dress as people dressed a century ago, a decade ago, a year ago? What is the 'standard' to go by?

It seems to me that differences in occupation, climate and personal need are the first considerations. But closely behind comes the importance of 'fitting in' with the people with whom one is in contact. This is especially important if one is a Christian, who really wants to communicate with other people; 'oddness' or incongruity of dress can erect petty but damaging barriers to communication.

Then one needs to consider comfort (including aesthetic and psychological comfort) and beauty. Creativity would be the next factor, as, in this area of clothing, some people have their 'hidden talent', their 'hidden art' which should be expressed and fulfilled. Some people have an ability for designing, cutting, sewing, tailoring, fitting, doing handwork, embroidering, knitting and crocheting, as well as weaving cloth in the first place! All these creative talents should be used, not buried: used in the midst of day-by-day inspirations and year-by-year changes. One can be original, and yet fit in with the general location and group – the place where God has chosen to put *you*.

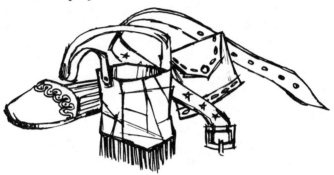

Can varieties of clothing, hair style, clean shaven face or beard, type of shoes or bare feet, be arbitrarily ruled to be spiritual or unspiritual, right or wrong? Surely not.

However, it is important to have a balanced, serious approach to all this. We are not to be dogmatic in rebellion, nor dogmatic in being conservative or 'straight'. The person with long hair should not be snobbish and reject the person with short hair. The person with bare feet should not scorn the person with shoes. The person without a hat should not segregate himself from the person with a hat. The person with gloves and a cane should not feel superior to the person with bare hands and a stick. The person with a completely beautiful blend of colours and fabrics, well chosen and international in fashion and 'correctness', should not be alienated from the person in clashing colours with no sense of beauty, cleanliness or even fragrance.

The thing of first importance is finding some sort of communication with the person *inside*: inside the hair, inside the hat, inside the blue jeans, inside the Paris dress, inside the shaven face or the beard. There is more to consider than the outward things, a fact the Bible stresses over and over. The cleanliness of the outside of the cup, if there are filthy germs inside, does not help much in sanitation! The beauty of dress and person, shining hair and glow of skin cannot assure one of the beauty of the character inside nor, incidentally, tell us anything as to whether that one has been inwardly cleansed from sin by Christ. So some serious thinking must take place in the area of our basic attitudes and our judgement of people must be free from superficiality.

But if we say that it is right to dress to 'fit in', we have to go on to ask, "Fit in with whom?"

My father went to China at the turn of the century, as a missionary under the China Inland Mission (now the Overseas Missionary Fellowship). At that time China could be better reached by missionaries dressing in Chinese dress, looking as much as possible like the Chinese, so that the message would be listened to, rather than the missionary simply being stared at as a curiosity, or being rejected as a 'foreign devil'. So missionaries wore native dress. For my mother this consisted of trousers and a high-collared Chinese robe made of a very lovely blue Chinese damask, frog buttoned down the side and embroidered. It would today be a very handsome evening trouser suit, very fashionable indeed! But at that time it was her way of fitting in with the people in the place where God had sent her to fulfil His purpose for her at that time. My father wore a long gown with very wide long sleeves and a stand-up collar. The frog closings were made of handsome twists of satin. Now some may say that a man should wear *men's* clothing. But a gown *was* men's clothing in that place, at that time. But there was more than that. Chinese men, at that moment in history, wore plaits. They had very very long hair, and braided it in a single braid that hung down their backs. The head was shaven in a circle so that no hair showed around the face. A black silk 'pill box' type of hat was worn, with a hole in the centre out of which the plait could come. Some missionaries bought ready-made plaits, and sewed them to the top of their hats. But my father disliked 'falseness' and grew his own hair. But—long hair for a man? The point was that at that time, and in that place, it 'fitted in' with the people to whom God had sent him. On the other hand, when Hudson Taylor walked down the streets of Victorian London with a plait, did that enhance him to the English of that time? Or, for that matter, if Jesus and the disciples suddenly walked into our churches, would someone mistake them for the 'wrong' sort of persons, simply on the grounds of their clothes and hair-style?

If God has taken you to a small town to farm, teach, preach, run the bank or even paint pictures, then your choice of clothing, style of your hair and general appearance of person is very important. Is your purpose simply to rebel against the 'stuffiness', or is there some willingness to blend in with the local custom? 'Blending' in this way does not need to be without originality and design, it does not rule out the exercise of taste and your own preference of fabrics and textures. If God has taken you to a very poor community to work among the underprivileged of that place, it is important not to flaunt riches, in the form of clothing, in a way that alienates you.

But even in dressing to 'fit in', one can use imagination in a way which is not only acceptable, but which may even inspire some of your friends with less money to make things themselves, and to 'save' in a new way, by being creative, instead of buying the cheap 'ready-mades'.

If God has taken you among very stylish people for some purpose of His, or among wealthy successful people, or among artistic, sophisticated people, it is not necessary nor helpful as a Christian to dress in a way which stands out like a sore thumb. One does not need jewels, costly furs, nor extravagant accessories to look not only well dressed, but beautifully and artistically dressed. The Christian should remember, wherever he is placed by the Lord, that he is not meant to 'put all his money on his back', nor selfishly to use his life to enhance his own looks and live in luxury, but he *is* the representative of a King – the King of Kings and Lord of Lords.

There is coming a day when we shall be 'dressed' by Him, as well as living in the mansions He is preparing. It is very important to be willing to sacrifice, and patiently to wait for that day. It is also very important to be modest, not to dress in such a way as to be mistaken for a bandit, a thief, or a prostitute; nor in such a way as to be a temptation to members of the other sex. However, keeping all these things in mind, it is still important to remember that we are representing the Creator of the universe and we are dressing for, and being dressed by, the One who tells us that even Solomon in all his glory was not dressed as magnificently as the flowers 'clothed' by Him.

A woman is described as virtuous in Proverbs. "She seeketh wool and flax, and worketh willingly with her hands . . . all her household are clothed with scarlet . . . She maketh herself coverings of tapestry; her clothing is silk and purple . . . She maketh fine linen . . ." Creativity, beauty and aesthetic taste are all employed in her own dressing and in the clothing of her family.

For anyone, man or woman, dress designing, dress making, designing of men's clothing, tailoring, making of children's clothes, and weaving the cloth to do it, does not have to be a career or life work and should not be an area of life where a person need be frustrated. There is nothing like knitting or sewing to give one the opportunity of using time in two ways at once. Perhaps you have to go to committee meetings which take a long time, board meetings or any meetings where you do not need to take notes, where your presence is required for votes and possible comments and where you really sit and listen and think without much to do with your hands. The time can be doubly well employed if you have some sewing, knitting or embroidery with you. The finished products give satisfaction too, both in the sheer fulfilment of accomplishment, and in the usefulness of the finished garment.

From my own experience of sewing, making my own and the children's clothing, I would say that nothing gives one the possibility of 'fitting in' with a wide variety of people like being able to

say, "I made it myself." To 'make it yourself' is to put your clothing, no matter how fashionable or plain, within the reach of each one with whom you have contact. If you yourself cannot sew perhaps your husband can. After all, the best tailors, and most of the big Paris dress designers, are men. It is not so surprising, then, that in our L'Abri family we have a fellow who has done brilliant work in his studies at Harvard, a concentrated intellectual who stops his studies for a time to "use my hands as a kind of relaxant", making clothes for his wife. He chooses the fabric, designs and cuts the dresses, stitches and does the hand work: in other words, he is creative in a 'Hidden Art' sort of manner.

Recently Jim has inspired tall, athletic Darrow to take up knitting, so if you visited L'Abri, you would not only see Barry and his helpers producing creative work with wood in the workshop, but at a lecture you might look twice to see who is crocheting and knitting! All we need now is a loom, or some silk worms.

Clothing

Christians all doing and acting the same? Christians all looking dowdy and seedy with their clothes the wrong cut and length? Somehow it doesn't seem to fit in with the flowers and all the rest of the amazing variety in God's creation. Flowers and sunsets, moon on water and delicate grasses in the starlight – would the designer of all this dress His own children, created in His image, in clothing which would make them unhappy and self-conscious? Would He have them all be alike and look alike?

What do you think?

13. Integration

"After this I beheld, and lo, a great multitude, which no man could number, of all nations, and kindreds, and people, and tongues, stood before the throne, and before the Lamb, clothed with white robes, and palms in their hands; And cried with a loud voice, saying, Salvation to our God which sitteth upon the throne, and unto the Lamb." "And they brought young children to him, that he should touch them: and his disciples rebuked those that brought them. But when Jesus saw it, he was much displeased, and said unto them, Suffer the little children to come unto me, and forbid them not: for of such is the kingdom of God."

Integration

These wonderful words, "All nations and kindreds and people and tongues" are among my favourite ones in the Bible. What a marvellous picture it conjures up of a gathering in which there is someone, or a number of people, from every single group of mankind, including many through the centuries of mankind who have been segregated from other groups by a dividing line of some description. Language has divided people: there is nothing so irritating as having other people chatter away in another tongue so that you have no clue what is being said. Language differences often bring about suspicion, misunderstanding and division. But at that future day, no longer will tongues divide. There will be a common tongue, an understanding that will be complete, a total communication that will include everyone. This will not be the partial understanding which comes with the learning of a new language, but real communication, an expressed oneness as all gather dressed alike in the white robes that are so significant in meaning and also in beauty. No one will be more beautifully dressed than another; there will be no possibility of anyone feeling proud or embarrassed; there will be a oneness of dress, and then in a oneness of voice, the multitude will say 'loudly' – not hesitantly, for fear of not believing or understanding the content of what is being said; not softly because of fearing one's accent might not be right; not fearing the voice will crack; but confidently and with all the assurance of being in the new body like Christ's glorious body, without hindrance of any kind – "Salvation to our God which sitteth upon the throne, and unto the Lamb." At that moment there will be a complete integration of languages, accomplished not by resolution but by God's changing us back to the condition we were in before the tower of Babel. Suddenly, instead of the confusion, there will be understanding and order, the perfect order of communication which is complete and total.

Everyone now will have the same thing in their hands. All who are there will be there for the same reason, not because they were 'good' on earth but because they have been forgiven and cleansed by the death of Christ, the Lamb, in their place. Everyone will have come with 'empty hands' in the sense of not having anything to bring to pay for salvation. But now there will be the integration of all doing the same thing at the same time, something we have never experienced perfectly in our life times. Nation has stood

against nation. Nation has fought against nation. War has continued and will continue right up to the end, Christ tells us. But in this heavenly gathering for all eternity, some from each warring nation of history will be together for ever. No nation will have been able to exclude people from another nation. Every single nation that has ever existed will be represented. The Messiah, who came through one nation, will, by His death, gather all the nations together in this way – some from each will be there.

The word 'kindred' speaks of family lines. 'Pride in the family tree', 'aristocrats', 'the lower classes', 'good blood', 'bad blood', 'royal family', 'slave background': what sort of separating lines have there been in every nation, as within the nations people have drawn themselves away from other people, with pride and with fear, with shame and with anger, with rebellion and revenge, with feuds and with hostility, with segregation of the most specific and cutting exactness? But, in this future day, all who have been born into the family of God will be one kindred. There will be no separation there, but a perfect integration into one family. Here is an integration such as man has never dreamed of.

In the other quotation from the Bible at the head of this chapter we read how Jesus became displeased with the disciples because they were trying on one occasion to segregate the children from the grown-ups. The disciples were displaying an attitude which regards adults as more important, while children needed to be brushed aside. Jesus was quite definite not only that children could come to Him but that the disciples had it all backwards. The adults need to come as the children come. It is the trust of a child for its father that is needed, the whole-hearted belief. All this, Jesus was teaching. However, this incident also adds something to our understanding of integration, when combined with the verse from Revelation. The future integration is to be an integration of *age* just as much as an integration of races and families. We put people into categories of age so easily but here we are told concerning children that "of such is the kingdom of heaven". Mentioning children in this way, and in this context, should give us a key to understanding what any truly complete gathering of the human race into one family is supposed to mean. A complete gathering when everything is perfect will be a gathering of some from every nation and kindred and people and tongue – and *age group*. Not only will children be included but every moment of human history will be included. Abraham will not be proud and draw himself away from us because he has been in existence so much longer! Paul will not feel he cannot speak to us because of his superior knowledge of theology and the deep truths of the faith. Enoch will not feel superior because he talked with God so long ago.

So, what is the 'right' age to be? Too young to know, too young to realize, too young to have had experience, too young to understand, too young to take responsibility? And then, suddenly, too old to be in tune with the modern generation, too old *really* to understand, too old to have 'kept up', too old to have the energy? It gets confusing at times, if one considers the matter, because it is very hard to discover just what the 'right age' might be, and how long it might last! I wrote a poem once expressing my thoughts on this confusion, and started it, "Age, age, how strange thou art, all the way from end to start!" And when you begin to consider eternity, and the fact that *personality* is endless you realize that Jeremiah, Daniel, David, Isaac, Timothy, Peter, Matthew, Zacchaeus and the rest are not going to be so much older and wiser than we so that we shall be hopelessly unable to catch up; nor is any one born after us going to be too young to 'understand' heaven and all the wonders of eternity.

Whatever 'age' people will be in heaven, whether there is gradual growth in children or whatever happens, we can know this, that there is to be an integration of ages there. We shall be there together from every kindred and nation and people and tongue, and from every historic age of the world's history and having entered heaven at every age of human life on earth. What an amazingly *complete* integration that will be! What an amazing scope of conversations we shall have!

What has all this to do with creative living, as a Christian? I feel it has a great deal to do with it. We live in a time when people are terribly segregated and becoming more segregated all the time. It is true that integration is the subject of conversations, lectures, school books, novels and newspapers, and is the content of laws and edicts. But I am talking about a more complete and true integration. It is not helping true integration to make laws.

Integration

True integration is a matter of people really feeling a oneness with others and attempting to understand them in personal communication of the sort that takes place around fireplaces, washing dishes together, having tea together, eating together, walking together, and discovering things in common together. True integration is a matter of people having spiritual communication and fellowship together, discussing and discovering new thoughts and ideas by sharing their trends of thought, or thinking out loud and having some kind of creative activities or recreation together – by choice, not law.

Who is segregated? Who needs to be integrated? Of course, nations and kindreds and people and tongues do. People who talk a different 'language' may all be speaking in the same basic language as far as linguistics go, but it may be a totally different 'language' philosophically speaking and so even within language groups, even within nations, even *within* kindred groups, there can be terrible 'segregation'.

To have a basis for real communication, giving a new kind of reality to creative possibilities among human beings, there needs to be a greater sharing. This can never be perfect on this earth, because the whole universe has been spoiled by sin. Yet there is scope for sharing our differences in understanding, viewpoint, background, experience. In heaven, in eternity, people will be bringing each other understanding of the *total* flow of history, because of each one bringing a personal understanding of their viewpoint and understanding of *their* moment of history. So during any one given moment of history, there would be greater understanding if people could only be in such a relationship with others that they could share experience and understanding.

How can 'Hidden Art' help to achieve this, in practical, everyday ways, fulfilling our talents and aspirations, our need for creative fulfilment, and so on?

In this area of 'Hidden Art', I feel that we should consider first of all the need for an integration of ages. And by that I mean an integration first of all within the family. Imagine a father of 42, a mother of 39, a daughter of 17, a son of 13, a little girl of 10, and a small boy of 5. Here is grandfather who is 73, and grandmother who is 69, and great-grandfather who is 95. Then there is Aunt Daisy who is 54, and Cousin Cynthia who is 35. There is enormous scope for integration here. How can 'Hidden Art' help to stimulate it?

Family occasions can be planned to include each member of the family; meals together during which the viewpoints and interests of the children are given a place and during which the world events discussed are not discussed as if the subject matter were high above their heads, with the adults being careful to explain, even to the five-year-old, what is being talked about. Opinions and reactions should be encouraged, so that there is a rich sharing of the 95-year-old viewpoint, with all the remembered years of past history to give flavour, and the 17-year-old viewpoint, with his contemporaries reflected in his remarks. There should be the female and male reaction listened to, each considering the other. Family gatherings can include the reading of books aloud, as an evening's entertainment together for all ages. There can be games, or new and original entertainment, or a new kind of guessing game. Whatever is planned and done, there should be the rich exchange of *ages* which nothing else can give.

One reason for the loss of family life today, I believe, is the incessant emphasis on dividing ages into tight categories. There are the kindergarten group, the juniors, the intermediates, the seniors, the young business people, the young married ones, the older married couples, and the 'senior citizens'. There are high school groups, college groups, university groups, and professional groups; everyone segregated from everyone else who is not the same age, and often of the same occupation! This seeps into the family unit, too, so that people just do not expect to enjoy each other or really communicate unless they are exactly the same age.

Integration

The family should be the place where an opposite trend is begun. Families ought to spend more time finding out how much fun it is to do things with a variety of ages, each contributing his or her originality and creative talent to the whole. The exchange would give a far wider understanding of life and people, and the present moment of history. Then the family unit could be added to from time to time, with some invited guests, not all of one age group, but each one bringing a friend into the whole group, for a dinner, a picnic or a Sunday High Tea, and conversations, book-reading, games and music, could be shared in this integrated atmosphere. I cannot understand the almost exclusive emphasis on racial integration, as if we were already integrated in other ways, when in fact we are getting more and more segregated into tight little cliques on age grounds.

This could be done on a wider basis also. In churches, Sunday schools, neighbourhoods and communities of various numbers of people, this trend could be started of getting people of a variety of ages to do things together, and communicate together. When you really get to know people, their hopes and fears, aspirations and disappointments, viewpoints and misunderstandings, there is a sympathy and a desire to help, a true compassion and love which begins to grow.

All this – age integration as well as integration of people of different nationalities, social backgrounds and educational backgrounds – will in itself give a new spurt of life to the veins of creativity! The tight little segregated life, always spent with people of your own age, economic group, educational background and culture tends to bring an ingrown, static sort of condition. Fresh ideas, reality of communication and shared experiences will be sparks to light up fires of creativity, especially if the people spending time together are a true cross-section of ages, nationalities, kindreds and tongues.

Just think of listening to someone who can tell you what it was like at the age of twelve to thrill over Lindbergh's flight across the ocean, and after hearing that remembered experience to turn and get the viewpoint of the 12-year-old who has just gone through the thrill of watching on television the first men to walk on the moon. Or think of someone telling of his first radio – the horn-shaped loud-speaker, the excitement of the early programmes – and then discussing the boy (for it was a 14-year-old boy who made this discovery) who wrote the formula on the blackboard for the first television. The experiences, viewpoints and conclusions of people are affected by the moment of history into which they are born. So why sterilize your life by keeping out all the germs of ideas born in another moment of history?

The same thing is true of geographical locations of birth and life. To exchange viewpoints and understanding with people who were born in Communist lands, who escaped under barbed wire, who went through war and famine; to hear something of life where there is no freedom, or to talk to someone born in a jungle, or in one of America's city jungles, is real education; while talking to scientists, doctors, dancers, farmers, milkmen, artists, writers, storekeepers, waiters, professors, and pastors gives you something no newspaper or book could give you.

But there is an art to conversation, to communication, to human relationships, an art to community living. There is an art to what is called in the Bible 'peacemaking', bringing together people of varied ages and backgrounds to help them to understand each other. This is a place where there is much scope for 'Hidden Art', and the 'canvas' for this 'painting' is the canvas of human relationships. You do not have to be a delegate to an international gathering on a large scale to *do* something. The most *real* 'something' you can do is within the family unit, as you open it up to others, to a cross-section of ages and peoples, or the gathering together of community life on a small scale.

L'Abri has developed along with this integration of an enormous variety of colour, language, nationality, occupation, education and age. The experience of fifteen years in seeing the cross-communication among people has been tremendous. It is far from perfect, but *something* is happening in lives. In the midst of much else, L'Abri attempts to explain what the twentieth century climate or atmosphere consists of, and where it came from; to give understanding to a cross-section of modern people; to provide a base from which to give truth from the biblical standpoint, and teaching which is full and rounded. It is not just a place to air ideas and viewpoints. But nevertheless there is an 'at-homeness' which people of widely different age-groups and from many different backgrounds seem to feel. To have a cross section of *ages* enjoying the community life is really significant in the twentieth century.

There is no real possibility of an integration that is true and meaningful in the total sense unless it is based on the inner integration which God has made possible through the Second Person of the Trinity, Jesus Christ. He died so that man might move out of his 'segregated' position, segregated from God, from other men, and even from himself in so many aspects, into a true integration. This true integration comes only when man is integrated with the Trinity. Jesus becomes one's Saviour, as one accepts that which He has done for man on the Cross. His death is not for 'mankind' as an impersonal whole but for each individual who accepts Him. God the Father becomes one's own Father at that time, and the Third Person of the Trinity, the Holy Spirit, indwells one, so one is truly integrated with the whole Trinity. When this has happened, a man can be helped by the Trinity to find at least the beginning of a true integration with other people. We can have help in understanding others, loving them and communicating with them. Now also we find a possibility of being more intergrated personalities. We have a base, a reference point, an atmosphere within which integration is possible. This is not simply a psychological trick. This is the real universe – it is coming into contact and communication with that which truly exists! This is a personal universe, in that the personal God does exist and He made it; and we have a split time of living in it, if we try to live as if it were impersonal.

It is no wonder that the big drive for integration seems so often to result in more active and violent segregation. It is quite a pathetic thing to see a child hit another over the head with a brick screaming, "Love me". The need is for this three-way integration: to keep from split personalities, split living as far as the real world goes, and split heads! What an area for creativity: moment by moment to do something about this, in personal living reality, not by impersonal law. In this lies the possibility of beauty in human relationships, which in fact exceeds the beauty of anything else within the scope of our creativity.

14. Environment

There is a fairly new art form called 'The Happening' or 'The Environment'. It is exhibited in various Art Museums, including the Stedelijk Museum in Amsterdam. I would say only here that 'The Environment' differs from other art forms in that instead of standing and looking at a picture of a statue in front of you and judging it, 'The Environment' involves a whole room, in turn created to involve *you* in thoughts and emotions as soon as you step into it. The idea is that you are involved in an environment which has an effect on you, drawing you into something the artist wants you to feel and think, rather than giving you an opportunity to observe and judge. If the environment is an immoral one, you are involved without having made a conscious choice at all.

This chapter within the framework of 'Hidden Art', however, is not dealing with new art, but a fresh understanding of an old truth. In thinking of 'The Environment' as an art form one thinks of a number of things. For instance, we all have been born into an environment that affects us, the environment of the twentieth century; and the kind of people we are, and are becoming, is affected by the moment of history into which we have been born and the degree of our acceptance of, or resistance to, the general trend.

But the idea of 'The Environment' brings other thoughts. After all we *are* an art form. I do not mean that we *produce* art consciously now, but I mean we *are* an art form, whether we think of it or not, and whether we do anything about it or not. We *are* an environment, each one of us. We are an environment for the other people with whom we live, the people with whom we work, the people with whom we communicate. And in this sense we do not choose an art form and create something in that form; we *are* an art form. Just as 'The Environment' created by modern artists in the museums involves people when they simply walk in, so we are an environment which is affecting people around us. People who come across us or who walk into our presence, become *involved*. There are various art forms we may or may not have talent for, may or may not have time for, and we may or may not be able to express ourselves in, but we ought to consider this fact - that whether we choose to be an environment or not, *we are*. We produce an environment other people have to live in. We should be conscious of the fact that this environment which we produce by our very 'being' can affect the people who live with us or work with us. The effect on them is something they cannot avoid. We should have thoughtfulness concerning our responsibility in this area. We should be artists in doing something about the environment we are creating – artists before God, of course. We have His help because we are artists in *this* sense, in the hands of the Holy Spirit; for if we are Christians, He is dwelling in us, and we can ask for His power to help us.

In the power of the Holy Spirit we can be an environment that is really an art form God can be using directly to affect and involve other people. Of course, we do not give the Holy Spirit perfect freedom to work in and through us because we hinder Him through sin and neglect. But it is an amazing thought that we are the art form God can use in this area of environment to involve others who come into our presence. Our conversations, attitudes, behaviour, response or lack of response, hardness or compassion, our love or selfishness, joy or dullness, our demonstrated trust and faith or our continual despondency, our concern for others or our self pity – all these things make a difference to the people who have to live in *our* 'environment'. Enthusiasm and excitement infect other people: expectancy that God can intervene and do something in this moment of history and doing something practical to *show* that expectancy in prayer, affects the attitudes other people are going to have to their troubles.

But it is not just aspects of your character, personality, attitudes or spiritual state which will affect the lives of others working or living by your side. It is also your appearance and the way you care for the things in the bedroom, the bathroom, and the kitchen!

It makes an enormous difference if someone creates an environment for you to live in. One person sleeps half the day, gets up looking like a half-dead duck, drags around with eyelids scarcely open, slurping coffee and leaving a mess all over the newly polished sink, leaves the bed unmade and a week of clothing in a heap on the bed, heaves a sigh and moans about what a drag life is, then

prepares to sit and philosophize while you work. What is the effect of this on you? Surely, you begin to feel tired, discouraged, irritated, frustrated and hopeless. Your own energy begins to ebb away. You decide to put off the rush of getting your article written. After all, you might as well go out for a walk. And so one wasted, ugly life infects another.

A second person gets up when the alarm goes off, or soon after, puts water on for the tea or coffee and helps to get breakfast, takes a bath and dresses so cheerily that you feel the sun must be shining and have to look again to realize the sky is still grey, makes his bed and clears things up so that you feel the urge to get to work soon, tidies the living room so that it looks better than it had been left the night before, and talks with an awareness and enthusiasm that gives you inspiration for your article and you feel there will be no doubt about getting it finished in time. Both have pitched into work before the hoped-for starting time, feeling a surge of accomplishment and energy that seems to multiply the time instead of wasting it.

Environment

There are room-mates who tidy and make their beds, and run a vacuum cleaner even when it is not their turn; but there are others who make the bedroom of six people a nightmare of a place, like sleeping in a slum.

When it is someone's special day – a long-awaited occasion – and guests have been invited and room-mate (or relative) number one wears old, torn clothing, or dirty jeans, when the 'someone' has washed his hair, and dressed in the best clothes he has, then the former is rather a dash of cold water on the festive air. More than that – he is insensitive to this whole matter of environment. It isn't 'square' or 'bourgeois' to notice that even if there were no people in the world to observe other than the one you are living with, such things as careful dressing, looking beautiful, artistic or original make an aesthetic difference to the person who wants to feel a 'special' atmosphere on this special occasion. Or perhaps it would be a help to imagine a wedding which has long been prepared for. The chapel is beautifully decorated with logs, moss, ivy, fern and chrysanthemums planted in hollow bricks standing on end and chrysanthemums tied with satin ribbon on every chair. Everyone has dressed in clean clothes, some very 'dressed up', others just clean, but all with a festive touch – a ribbon or a flower in the hair, some mark of celebration having been made. Then in comes a couple in dirty clothes, muddy boots, uncombed hair. They get mud all over the aisle as they walk up, knock the flowers and ribbon off a couple of chairs, and sit down with feet sticking out in the aisle. Are they living simply with 'freedom', 'unto themselves', affecting no one? No, the bride's dress gets dirty as the train sweeps the mud; the lovely line of chrysanthemums she had dreamt of walking between has empty spots and a couple of torn stray flowers on the floor. The moment of beauty has been spoiled. It is all right if the other couple want a wedding without beauty of dress, flower, moss or fern. It is all right if they want to be without beauty around them. But the freedom of the first couple has been destroyed by two who have no notion that they themselves are an art form, an environment which involves other people who have had no chance to make a choice about it.

Jesus told a story of a man who tried to attend a wedding without putting on the prescribed wedding garment. What an environment he would be to the others, were he allowed to go in! The story is intended, of course, to illustrate that no-one can go to heaven without the 'wedding garment', the white linen robe of the righteousness of Christ. In other words, we need to be covered with His righteousness, rather than our sins. We cannot go to heaven in our filthy rags of sin, but as Jesus died He not only washed the rags away but provided us with 'white linen gowns' instead. He has prepared the garment for us, by living a sinless life. So God is specific about the *environment* of heaven; no spot, no dirt, no sin is to enter in to spoil it. That environment is protected. We will not be involved in sin or temptation there. There will be no Satan to bedraggle our gowns.

However, here in this life, a Christian should *be* an environment which is helpful to the people with whom he lives. This is not just a matter of dress and tidiness but also of character and spiritual life. It is worth considering what sort of an 'art form' we are. What sort of an environment do we drag in with us? How do we affect other people in their attitudes toward that which we are supposed to represent?

We are either being what the Holy Spirit would have us be, or we are hindering His work in us and through us. As God created the world, He was creating an environment for man which, we are told, was 'good'. In each thing that God created, each art form He brought forth, "He saw that it was good". It was a good environment before sin entered to spoil it. But Christians, who are restored to relationship and fellowship with God, should ask that they might be an environment that is conducive to others wanting to come to God.

Sacrifice? Yes! Of course, we must be willing to have little, to live in frugal conditions, to have no 'security' financially and to depend utterly upon God to supply what would enable us to do His will. But sacrifice does not mean ugliness, nor does it mean carelessness. There is no place where one cannot plant ivy over the mud hut and put a flower on the stump. There is nowhere in the world where it is not important to remember that we not only must be thoughtful of beauty, but also thoughtful in the area of our own responsibilities as an environment.

There were some Africans who were with us a couple of years ago, who sat in our bedroom talking to my husband before they left. Each of them had been in some sort of a mission school and now were in European universities on scholarships. Each of them at some time or another had come into the homes of missionaries and had observed various things during their boyhood. They each made a similar comment which impressed me deeply. Each of them said that the thing which had turned them away from Christianity was the lack of beauty in the missionaries' homes – and they were speaking of physical beauty. I have no idea of the name of the towns nor any idea of what mission they were referring to, let alone individuals, so this is simply anonymous!

It was a sobering thing to us to find that these boys had all observed the same thing and were describing how it affected them. Here were these bright young Africans saying that the missionaries who had come to their countries had had no beauty in their homes.

Now I am sure that if you had talked to any of these missionaries they would have been astonished that these young boys had made such observations. I am sure they would have felt that they had a 'standard of living' much higher than the people among whom they worked. They would have been astonished at the sensitivity to beauty, and at the sharpness of the criticism, and at the resultant turning away from Christianity which these boys linked with the lack of beauty.

I am sure that there is no place in the world where your message would not be enhanced by your making the place (whether tiny or large, a hut or a palace) orderly, artistic and beautiful with some form of creativity, some form of 'art'. It goes without saying, too, that 'The Environment', which is *you* should be an environment which speaks of the wonder of the Creator who made you.